CHRISTIAN THEOLOGY AND ISLAM

The Pro Ecclesia Series

Books in The Pro Ecclesia Series are "for the Church." The series is sponsored by the Center for Catholic and Evangelical Theology, founded by Carl Braaten and Robert Jenson in 1991. The series seeks to nourish the Church's faithfulness to the gospel of Jesus Christ through a theology that is self-critically committed to the biblical, dogmatic, liturgical, and ethical traditions that form the foundation for a fruitful ecumenical theology. The series reflects a commitment to the classical tradition of the Church as providing the resources critically needed by the various churches as they face modern and post-modern challenges. The series will include books by individuals as well as collections of essays by individuals and groups. The Editorial Board will be drawn from various Christian traditions.

CURRENT TITLE:

The Morally Divided Body: Ethical Disagreement and the Disunity of the Church (2012), edited by Michael Root and James J. Buckley

FORTHCOMING TITLES INCLUDE:

Who Do You Say That I Am? Proclaiming and Following Jesus Today, edited by Michael Root and James J. Buckley

What Does It Mean to "Do This"? Supper, Mass, Eucharist, edited by Michael Root and James J. Buckley

Heaven, Hell, . . . and Purgatory?, edited by Michael Root and James J. Buckley

Christian Theology and Islam

edited by

Michael Root &
James J. Buckley

CASCADE *Books* • Eugene, Oregon

CHRISTIAN THEOLOGY AND ISLAM

The Pro Ecclesia Series 2

Cascade Books
An Imprint of Wipf and Stock Publishers
199 W. 8th Ave., Suite 3
Eugene, OR 97401

www.wipfandstock.com

ISBN 13: 978-1-61097-814-9

Cataloging-in-Publication data:

Christian theology and Islam / edited by Michael Root and James J. Buckley.

x + 120 p. ; 23 cm. —Includes bibliographical references.

The Pro Ecclesia Series 2

ISBN 13: 978-1-61097-814-9

1. Christianity and other religions—Islam. 2. Islam—Relations—Christianity. I. Root, Michael, 1951–. II. Buckley, James J. III. Title. IV. Series.

BP172 .C4198 2014

Manufactured in the U.S.A.

Contents

Contributors

James J. Buckley is Professor of Theology at Loyola University Maryland. He has contributed to and edited (with Frederick Bauerschmidt and Trent Pomplun) *The Blackwell Companion to Catholicism* (2007). He is an associate director of the Center for Catholic and Evangelical Theology.

David B. Burrell, CSC, Theodore Hesburgh Professor Emeritus in Philosophy and Theology at the University of Notre Dame, currently serves the Congregation of Holy Cross as consultant to the new Notre Dame University of Bangladesh in Dhaka. Efforts since 1982 in comparative issues in philosophical theology in Judaism, Christianity, and Islam are evidenced in *Knowing the Unknowable God: Ibn-Sina, Maimonides, Aquinas* (1986), *Freedom and Creation in Three Traditions* (1993), *Original Peace* (with Elena Malits,1998), and *Friendship and Ways to Truth* (2000), as well as two translations: *Al-Ghazali on the Ninety-Nine Beautiful Names of God* (1993) and *Al-Ghazali on Faith in Divine Unity and Trust in Divine Providence* (2001); and more recently, essays exploring *Faith and Freedom* (2004) and *Learning to Trust in Freedom* (2009), as well as a theological commentary on Job, *Deconstructing Theodicy* (2008).

Nelly van Doorn-Harder is Professor of Islamic Studies at Wake Forest University. She was trained in the Netherlands and received her PhD from the Free University of Amsterdam. Her research straddles issues concerning women and religion and those concerning minorities, minority cultures, human rights in Muslim countries, and the interreligious encounter between Muslims and Christians. She has done her main fieldwork in the Middle East and Southeast Asia, specializing in indigenous Christianity of Egypt and Indonesian Islam. Among the books she has authored are *Contemporary Coptic Nuns* (1995), *Women Shaping Islam: Indonesian Muslim Women Reading the Qur'an* (2006), and (with Magdi Guirguis) *The*

Emergence of the Modern Coptic Papacy (2011). Currently her primary area of research concerns Muslim spirituality in Southeast Asia.

Sidney H. Griffith is Ordinary Professor in the Department of Semitic and Egyptian Languages and Literatures at The Catholic University of America, with responsibilities in Syriac and Christian Arabic. His most recent book is *The Church in the Shadow of the Mosque: Christians and Muslims in the World of Islam* (2010).

Sandra Keating is Associate Professor of Theology at Providence College. She has published numerous articles and a book on relations between Muslims and Catholics, with a particular emphasis on theological exchange in the medieval period. Among others, she is a member of the USCCB Catholic-Muslim dialogue group, and she has served on the Vatican Commission for Religious Relations with Muslims. She lives in Rhode Island with her husband, Jim, and two children.

Rick Love holds a ThM in New Testament studies and a DMin in urban studies from Westminster Theological Seminary, and a PhD in intercultural studies from Fuller Theological Seminary. He is president of Peace Catalyst International and serves as a consultant for Christian-Muslim relations.

Michael Root is Professor of Systematic Theology at The Catholic University of America and Executive Director of the Center for Catholic and Evangelical Theology. He was formerly the Director of the Institute for Ecumenical Research, Strasbourg, France.

Mark N. Swanson is the Harold S. Vogelaar Professor of Christian-Muslim Studies and Interfaith Relations at the Lutheran School of Theology at Chicago; previously he taught at Luther Seminary in St. Paul, Minnesota (1998–2006), and at the Evangelical Theological Seminary in Cairo, Egypt (1984–1998). A Lutheran pastor who holds a doctorate from the Pontifical Institute for Arabic and Islamic Studies, he is a student of Arabic Christian literature, early Christian-Muslim encounter, and medieval Coptic Orthodox church history.

Introduction

The goal of the following chapters is to address the question: how can Christians committed to the classical Christian tradition (Evangelicals and Catholics) address the issues raised by contemporary Islam? The goal, we emphasize, is not Christian-Muslim dialogue—as worthy as that goal certainly is. Along with and even prior to such dialogue Christians need to ask themselves how their Scriptures and traditions might bear on such dialogue. Do the divisions among Christians (Catholic and Evangelical) fracture the classical Christian tradition in ways that undercut "Christian"-Muslim dialogue before it starts? Or does that classical tradition provide resources for thinking out and working out their own divisions in ways that will ready them for authentic conversation with Muslim brothers and sisters in Christ? And what does this tradition have to teach us about what Christians can and must learn from Muslims about their own traditions?

The essays are organized as a movement from the historical through the contemporary. Historically we begin prior to the modern era, prior to the Reformation, and even prior to the medieval Crusades. Instead we begin with the Muslim-Christian engagement prior to the first millennium, when Islam's Qur'an had emerged and Christians were emerging from their battles at the first ecumenical councils. We do this not because we think that these other eras of Muslim-Christian engagement and non-engagement are unimportant (although many Western historians nowadays seem to think that "the Crusades" have been more important for Christians than for Muslims until recently).[1] Instead we wager that these earliest encounters can help us attend to issues that we have thus far not noticed.

Sidney Griffith guides us in a journey on the way early Christian theologians from diverse and sometimes competing traditions articulated the doctrine of the triune God in conversation with the Islamic Qur'an,

1. "The simple fact is that the crusades were virtually unknown in the Muslim world even a century ago." Thomas F. Madden, *The New Concise History of the Crusades* (Oxford: Rowan & Littlefield, 2006) 217.

learning from Islamic traditions even as they disagreed about the unity and trinity of God. Sandra Keating focuses on a single Christian Arabic theologian for whom Muslims as well as Christians are participants in God's ongoing pedagogy in Christ and the Spirit. Mark Swanson concentrates the concerns of Griffith and Keating on the question of whether early Christian arguments for true religion are evasions of authentic accounts for the hope that is in us, rather than "apologetic portfolios" with crucial lessons for us today.

These historical theologians provide a context in which to read Christians with contemporary philosophical and pastoral interests. David Burrell reminds us that Christian engagement of Islam is inseparable from our engagement with Judaism—and that these Abrahamic faiths share the mystery of the free Creator-creature relation, even as they differ on the eternal Torah, the Word made flesh, or the Qur'anic word made Arabic as the patterns for the Creator-creature relation. Rick Love explores the stereotypical rivalry between peacemakers and evangelists and then constructs a biblical theology of "peacemaking and respectful witness," particularly as a guide for Christians working with Muslims in concrete situations in Nigeria or Central Java today. Nelly van Doorn-Harder seeks for new grassroots interfaith engagements, and describes how concrete initiatives taken by Indonesian Muslims and Christians can provide models to take us beyond the theological and political impasses.

We are trying to suggest one way these diverse essays share a common agenda rather than trying to summarize essays readers can assess for themselves. The agenda is clearly unfinished, and we invite readers to discern the similarities as well as differences in the agenda proposed. The essays were originally presented at a 2008 Conference on Christian Theology and Islam sponsored by the Center for Catholic and Evangelical theology. The center has been sponsoring such conferences since its founding in 1991 by Robert Jenson and Carl Braaten. Our goal is not only to sponsor timely gatherings on Catholic and Evangelical theology but also to bring together pastors and academics, biblical exegetes and homilists, historians and theologians interested in faithfulness to the gospel of Jesus Christ throughout the churches. We are delighted that these essays are among the first in the Pro Ecclesia Series.

Michael Root and James J. Buckley

1

The Unity and Trinity of God

Christian Doctrinal Development in Response to the Challenge of Islam—An Historical Perspective

Sidney H. Griffith

I

The first and most insistent article of Islamic faith is expressed in the familiar formula of the first phrase of the *shahādah*, the ritual testimony that "there is no god but God," a phrase that in these exact words appears only twice in the Qur'ān (XXXVII *aṣ-Ṣāffāt* 35 and XLVII *Muḥammad* 19); but it is echoed some forty times in the Islamic scripture's constant refrain, in various wordings, that "there is no god but He."[1] Further, the Qur'ān insists that God is one, with no consort, no offspring, no partner, and no

1. See Andrew Rippin, "Witness to Faith," in *Encyclopaedia of the Qur'ān*, ed. Jane Dammen McAuliffe, 5 vols. (Leiden: Brill, 2001–2006) 5:488–91. See also Anton Baumstark, "Zur Herkunft der monotheistischen Bekenntnisformeln im Koran," *Oriens Christianus* 37 (1953) 6–22, who searches for an ultimately Jewish or Samaritan liturgical formula behind the several Arabic phrases.

associate. The text insists that God is one God (*Allāh al-wāḥid*): "Your God is surely one" (XXXVII *aṣ-Ṣāffāt* 4); "He has no associate" (*lā sharīka lahu*, VI *al-an'ām* 163).

Accordingly, "to acknowledge that God is one" (*at-tawḥīd*) expresses the central doctrine of Islam, and to deny or compromise this acknowledgment is to commit the fundamental sin of *ash-shirk*, that is, to allege that God somehow has an associate; in Islamic terms it is the radical blasphemy, an ungrateful act of disbelief (*al-kufr*).[2] And so, in a particularly succinct and striking passage, the Qur'ān commands:

> Say, He is God, one [*aḥad*], God the everlasting. He does not beget; He is not begotten; there is not one like Him. (CXII *al-Ikhlāṣ* 1–4)

While it is true that in the milieu in which the Qur'ān most likely made its first appearance this passage may have been intended to rebut the beliefs of those Arabian polytheists who spoke of the sons and daughters of God, on the face of it the wording can just as well be taken to reject the doctrines of the Christians (*an-Naṣārā*) who say, according to the Qur'ān, "The Messiah is the son of God; that is what they say with their mouths; they imitate the saying of those who disbelieved earlier, may God fight them, how perverted they are" (IX *at-Tawbah* 30). It seems clear in fact from this verse that in the Qur'ān's view, what the Christians mistakenly say about Jesus the Messiah is what leads them to speak of "three" in connection with what they say about the "one" God.

There are only two verses in the Qur'ān that explicitly mention what we might call the "Christian three," and they do so in connection with a strong critique of what Christians say about Jesus. The most comprehensive verse reads as follows:

> O People of the Book, do not go beyond the bounds in your religion and do not say about God anything but the truth. The Messiah, Jesus, Mary's son, is only God's messenger, and His word, which He imparted to Mary, and a spirit from Him. So believe in God and His messengers, and do not say "three"; stop it, it is better for you. God is only one God [*ilāhun wāḥidun*], praised be He;

2. For a discussion of these matters, with an ample bibliography, see Gerhard Böwering, "God and His Attributes," in McAuliffe, *Encyclopaedia of the Qur'an*, 2:316–31. For more on the concept of *ash-shirk*, see G. R. Hawting, *The Idea of Idolatry and the Emergence of Islam: From Polemic to History* (Cambridge: Cambridge University Press, 1999) esp. 67–87; for more on the concept of *al-kufr*, see Toshihiko Izutsu, *Ethico-Religious Concepts in the Qur'ān* (Montreal: McGill University Press, 1966) esp. 119–77.

He has no child, His are what is in the heavens and what is on the earth. God is a sufficient one to trust. (IV *an-Nisā* 171)

On the face of it, the "three" that this verse commands the Christians to stop acknowledging are God, His word, and a spirit from Him, understood by the Christians, according to the Qur'ān, as one God with two "associates."[3] The Qur'ān makes the same point more obliquely in the only other passage in which there is an explicit mention of the "Christian three," where again the immediate reference is to Jesus the Messiah. The Qur'ān says: "They have disbelieved [*kafara*] who say that God is 'one of three'/'third of three' [*thālith thalāthatin*]. There is no God but one God. If they do not stop saying it, a grievous punishment will certainly befall those who have disbelieved" (V *al-Mā'idah* 73). While there is some discussion about the exact sense of the expression, in the context of the associated verses, the phrase "one of three"/"third of three" is clearly presented as an epithet of Jesus the Messiah;[4] the previous verse provides almost an exact parallel: "They have disbelieved who say God is the Messiah, the son of Mary. The Messiah said, O Sons of Israel, worship God, my Lord and your Lord; whoever gives God an associate [*man yushrik billāhi*], God has forbidden him the Garden and his abode will be the Fire" (V *al-Mā'idah* 72).

These verses from the Qur'ān, especially IV *an-Nisā* 171, suggest in so many words that the Qur'ān commands the Christians not to speak of the one God as God/Father, Word/Son, and Spirit. While over the centuries some scholars, both Muslim and Christian, citing yet another verse, have suggested that the Qur'ān envisions a Christian Trinity of God/Father, God/Mother/Mary, and Jesus/Son, the present writer has proposed elsewhere that this interpretation is wrong and that in the Islamic exegetical tradition it actually rests on a misunderstanding of the significance of the Qur'ānic epithet "one of three"/"third of three" quoted above.[5] Here is not the place to pursue the matter further; suffice it to say that in early Islamic times both Christian and Muslim scholars alike understood the Qur'ān's constant

3. See Matthias Radscheit, "Word of God," in McAuliffe, *Encyclopaedia of the Qur'an*, 5:541–48; Sidney H. Griffith, "Holy Spirit," in McAuliffe, *Encyclopaedia of the Qur'an*, 2:442–44.

4. See the discussion in Sidney H. Griffith, "Syriacisms in the Arabic Qur'ān: Who Were 'Those Who Said 'Allāh Is Third of Three' according to *al-Mā'idah* 73?" in *A Word Fitly Spoken: Studies in Mediaeval Exegesis of the Hebrew Bible and the Qur'ān Presented to Haggai Ben-Shammai*, ed. Meir M. Bar-Asher et al. (Jerusalem: Ben-Zvi Institute, 2007) 83–110.

5. See Griffith, "Syriacisms in the Arabic Qur'ān."

affirmation that God is one (*at-tawḥīd*)[6] to be directed against the contrary Christian affirmation that the one God is also three (*at-tathlīth*):[7] Father, Son, and Holy Spirit. For this reason, the earliest Muslim anti-Christian polemicists accused the Christians of effectively professing tritheism, while the earliest Christian apologists and anti-Islamic polemicists who lived in the Islamic world and wrote in Arabic accused the Muslims of missing the point of the Christian confession and of not following the logic of their own Islamic scripture, which, according to these Christian writers, clearly speaks of God, of God's Word, and of a Spirit from Him (IV *an-Nisā* 171).

Outside of the Qur'ān, the oldest surviving Islamic challenge to the propriety and veracity of the Christian doctrine of the Trinity is doubtless to be found in the long Arabic inscription placed just above the arches, on both sides of the inner octagonal arcade of the Dome of the Rock in Jerusalem.[8] Modern scholars have accepted the opinion that this inscription actually dates from the time of the original construction of the dome, at the behest and with the patronage of the caliph 'Abd al-Malik (685–705); the inscription itself mentions the year 691.[9] While the text on the outer face of the arcade is composed of brief phrases from the Qur'ān attesting that God is one and Muḥammad is God's prophet, the more accessible and easier to read text on the inner face of the arcade, facing the rock below, addresses the "People of the Book," that is, the Christians, in a clear polemical tone. Christel Kessler says of it:

6. See D. Gimaret, "Tawḥīd," in *Encyclopedia of Islam*, new ed., 10:389.

7. See D. Thomas, "Tathlīth," in *Encyclopedia of Islam*, new ed., 10:373–75. It is difficult accurately and felicitously to translate the Arabic infinitive (*maṣdar*) *tathlīth* into English; the most literal rendering might be "to trine" or "trining," "to treble" or "trebling," "to triplicate" or "triplicating," all of them awkward or misleading. So, one uses a phrase like "acknowledging" or "affirming" three.

8. On this monumental structure and its extraordinary significance, see Oleg Grabar, *The Shape of the Holy: Early Islamic Jerusalem* (Princeton: Princeton University Press, 1996); and, more popularly, Oleg Grabar, *The Dome of the Rock* (Cambridge: Harvard University Press, 2006).

9. See the detailed study and careful transcription of Christel Kessler, "'Abd al-Malik's Inscription in the Dome of the Rock: A Reconstruction," *Journal of the Royal Asiatic Society* (1970) 2–14. A revisionist reading of the inscription that has so far found few supporters is proposed by Christoph Luxenberg, "Neudeutung der arabischen Inschrift im Felsendom zu Jerusalem," in *Die dunklen Anfänge: Neue Forschungen zur Entstehung und frühen Geschichte des Islam*, ed. Karl-Heinz Ohlig and Gerd-Rüdiger Puin (Berlin: Schiler, 2005) 124–47.

> Here the proclamation of God's unity and Muḥammad's mission is followed by Qur'ānic verses, which address the "People of the Book," admonish them to make no mistake in their religion, denounce the idea of the Trinity (always understood as a kind of deviation from monotheism), and expound the proper view of Jesus as spirit of God, His word conveyed into Mary, and as nothing else than a true servant of God and His messenger. Therefore, what distinguishes the text on the interior from the text on the exterior is evidently the particular polemic intention.[10]

And in Jerusalem, on a seventh-century sight line extending from the Dome of the Rock westward to the Church of the Resurrection (the Church of the Holy Sepulcher), the inscription's Islamic proclamation makes explicit the dome's monumental counterclaim to the church's announcement of Christian faith, at the same time as it claims the authority of the public space of the Holy City for Islam.[11]

In later times, certainly from the ninth century onward, in their discussions of *at-tawḥīd*, Muslim theologians and philosophers regularly criticized the Christian doctrine of the Trinity, with greater or lesser understanding of the doctrine as the Christians actually professed it, depending on the level of awareness of the particular scholar.[12] Some were reasonably well informed about Christian teachings—scholars such as Abū 'Īsā al-Warrāq (d. c. 860),[13] or the Mu'tazilite 'Abd al-Jabbār al-Hamdhānī (d. 1025)[14]—but others, like Abū Manṣūr Muḥammad al-Māturīdī (d. 944),

10. Kessler, "'Abd al-Malik's Inscription," 11.

11. See Heribert Busse, "Die arabischen Inschriften im und am Felsendom," *Deutscher Verein vom Heiligen Land, Das Heilige Land* 118 (1977) 8–24. See also the unconvincing counterclaims of Luxenberg, "Der arabischen Inschrift," 140–46, who interprets the inscription as expressing not an Islamic critique of Christian doctrine, but a non-Trinitarian, pre-Nicene, Syro-Aramaic Christian faith, and who proposes that the dome was originally a Christian, not an Islamic shrine.

12. For Muslim, anti-Christian texts in the early Islamic period, see Ali Bouamama, *La littérature polémique musulmane contre le christianisme depuis ses origines jusqu'au XIIIe siècle* (Algiers: Enterprise Nationale du Livre, 1988); Jean-Marie Gaudeul, *Encounters and Clashes: Islam and Christianity in History*, 2 vols., rev. ed. (Rome: PISAI, 2000).

13. See David Thomas, *Anti-Christian Polemic in Early Islam: Abū 'Īsā al-Warrāq's "Against the Trinity,"* University of Cambridge Oriental Publications 45 (Cambridge: Cambridge University Press, 1992). See also the discussion of Abū 'Īsā in Dominique Urvoy, *Les penseurs libres dans l'Islam classique:L'interrogation sur la religion chez les penseurs arabes independents* (Paris: Michel, 1996) 102–17.

14. See, for example, Abū al-Hasan 'Abd al-Jabbār, *Al-Mughnī fī abwāb at-tawḥīd wa l-'adl*, 14 vols. in 16 (Cairo: Wizārat al-Thaqāfah wa l-Irshād al-Qawmī, al-Idārah

construed Christian doctrine entirely in Islamic terms that would scarcely have been intelligible to contemporary Christians.[15] But for the most part, the earliest surviving texts in evidence of Christian/Muslim controversy about the Trinity during the formative period of Islamic thought were written by Christians.

II

The systematic defense of the credibility of the doctrine of the Trinity against the objections of Muslims was a staple in the theological treatises written by Christians in Syriac and Arabic in the heady era of the burgeoning of classical Islamic intellectual culture, the period roughly contemporary with the famed Graeco-Arabic translation movement in Abbasid times, from the middle of the eighth century to the middle of the eleventh century.[16] During this time, Christian thinkers elaborated what would become the standard articulation of Trinitarian theology in Arabic, scarcely to be surpassed in later centuries, albeit that many later writers would contribute refinements to the traditional modes of discourse.

Arabic-speaking Christian writers employed a number of genres in their apologetic efforts in the Islamic milieu to commend the reasonableness of the basic articles of the Christian creed; some were addressed to a popular audience and some were intended for more philosophically or theologically inclined readers. In both instances, the writers took their cues from the critiques of Christian doctrines and practices that circulated in the common parlance of the Islamic world.[17] One supposes that the intended audiences were primarily Christians who, in the face of the

al-ʿAmmah lil-Thaqāfah, 1960–) 5:80–151. See also Gabriel Said Reynolds, *A Muslim Theologian in a Sectarian Milieu: ʿAbd al-Jabbār and the Critique of Christian Origins*, Islamic History and Civilization, Studies and Texts 56 (Leiden: Brill, 2004).

15. See Sidney H. Griffith, "Al-Māturīdī on the Views of the Christians: Readings in the *Kitāb at-Tawḥīd*," to appear in the Festschrift für Stefan Gerö.

16. See Dimitri Gutas, *Greek Thought, Arabic Culture: The Graeco-Arabic Translation Movement in Baghdad and Early ʿAbbasid Society (2nd–4th/8th–10th Centuries)* (London: Routledge, 1998).

17. See Georg Graf, "Christliche Polemik gegen den Islam," *Gelbe Hefte* 2 (1926) 825–42, reprinted in Georg Graf, *Christlicher Orient und schwäbische Heimat: Kleine Schriften*, ed. Hubert Kaufhold, 2 vols., Beiruter Texte und Studien 107 a & b (Beirut: Orient-Institut Beirut, ErgonVerlag Würzburg in Kommission, 2005) 2:587–602; Sidney H. Griffith, *The Church in the Shadow of the Mosque: Christians and Muslims in the World of Islam* (Princeton: Princeton University Press, 2008) 75–105.

Islamic critique, wanted reassurances about the credibility of their faith, and occasional Muslim readers, for whom the texts in Arabic would by the nature of the case be easily accessible. Some Muslims are even on record as having actually written refutations of the works of several Christian writers.[18] But the Christians in the Islamic world were not themselves a single community; they professed different ecclesial allegiances largely based on differing Christologies inherited from the church-dividing controversies of the immediately preceding, pre-Islamic times.[19] Indeed the several Christian communities carried these controversies with them into Islamic times, and their "denominations," if we may so call their divided communities, came into the full articulation of their distinctive identities only in Islamic times; the Muslims regularly called them "Melkites," "Jacobites," and "Nestorians," including under these names a number of other communities such as the Copts, the Armenians, and even the Maronites.[20] Nevertheless, while their theologies, and especially their Christologies, were in conflict with one another, these same Christians often insisted that they shared the same faith, albeit that they expressed it in differing and opposing confessional formulae.[21] However, in the matter of the doctrine of the Trinity and its defense in Arabic, the Christian apologists of all three communities were for the most part on the same page; all of them were faced with the task of convincingly commending the credibility of the Nicaeno-Constantinopolitan doctrine of one God, one divine being or substance (*ousia*), in three divine *hypostases* (*qnômê* in Syriac) or three divine "persons."[22]

18. See Griffith, *Church in the Shadow*, 99–103.

19. Currently the best single reference source for these communities, their doctrines, and their histories is Wolfgang Hage, *Das orientalische Christentum*, Religionen der Menschheit 29,2 (Stuttgart: Kohlhammer, 2007). See also Jean-Pierre Valognes, *Vie et mort des chrétiens d'Orient: Des origines à nos jours* (Paris: Fayard, 1994).

20. See Griffith, *Church in the Shadow*, 129–40. See also Martin Tamcke, *Christen in der islamischen Welt: Von Mohammed bis zur Gegenwart* (München: Beck, 2008).

21. See Griffith, *Church in the Shadow*, 140–42.

22. For an overview of the topic in Arab Christian texts, see Rachid Haddad, *La trinité divine chez les théologiens arabes (750–1050)*, Beauchesne Religions 15 (Paris: Beauchesne, 1985); Paul Khoury, *Matériaux pour server à l'étude de la controverse théologique de langue arabe du VIIIe au XIIe siècle*, Religionswissenschaftliche Studien 11,1–4 (Würzburg & Altenberge: Echter Verlag & Oros Verlag, 1989–1999) vol. 4, ch. 4, "Dieu un et trine." See also David Thomas, "The Doctrine of the Trinity in the Early Abbasid Era," in *Islamic Interpretations of Christianity*, ed. Lloyd Ridgeon (New York: St. Martin's, 2001) 78–98; Mark N. Swanson, "The Trinity in Christian-Muslim Conversation," *Dialog: A Journal of Theology* 44 (2005) 256–63.

For the present purpose, namely, the effort to present the general lines along which developments in Trinitarian theology took place at the hands of Arabic-speaking theologians living in the early Islamic milieu, while almost every apologetic or polemical text in every genre addressed the topic, the most fruitful works to study would be a selection of those treatises intended for the more philosophically and theologically inclined readers. In them we may discern the lines of theological development most clearly. In general, the writers followed apologetic trajectories designed to respond to challenges coming from three particular sets of Islamic discourse: scriptural testimony; the burgeoning *'ilm al-kalām*, what we might call Islamic "systematic theology"; and philosophical logic. Needless to say, all three trajectories were intertwined in the works of most writers, but here, for the sake of greater clarity, we shall discuss the approach to the defense of the credibility of the doctrine of the Trinity as it appears in the treatises of three particular writers, each of whose treatises may be taken to exemplify a particular apologetic trajectory. The writers are an anonymous "Melkite" apologist of the second half of the eighth century; an early Christian *Mutakallim* who flourished in the mid-ninth century, the "Nestorian" 'Ammār al-Baṣrī (fl. 850); and the "Jacobite" logician and theologian Yaḥyā ibn 'Adī (893–974).

A. Scriptural Testimony

As it happens, the earliest known apology for Christianity originally written in Arabic is an anonymous work by a "Melkite" writer to which its first modern editor gave the title, *On the Triune Nature of God.*[23] Subsequent studies have expanded our knowledge of this important work, allowing one the opportunity now to review it more accurately from the point of view of its interface with the challenge of Islam, and particularly with the Qur'ān.[24]

23. Margaret Dunlop Gibson, *An Arabic Version of the Acts of the Apostles and the Seven Catholic Epistles, with a Treatise on the Triune Nature of God*, Studia Sinaitica 7 (London: Clay, 1899) 74–107 (Arabic), 2–36 (English trans.).

24. See Samir Khalil Samir, "The Earliest Arab Apology for Christianity (c. 750)," in *Christian Arabic Apologetics during the Abbasid Period (750–1258)*, ed. Samir Khalil Samir and Jørgen S. Nielsen (Leiden: Brill, 1994) 57–114; Maria Gallo (trans.), *Palestinese anonimo: Omelia arabo-cristiana dell'VIII secolo* (Rome: Città Nuova, 1994); Mark N. Swanson, "Apologetics, Catechesis, and the Question of Audience in 'On the Triune Nature of God' (Sinai Arabic 154) and Three Treatises of Theodore Abū Qurrah," in *Christians and Muslims in Dialogue in the Islamic Orient of the Middle Ages:*

The treatise discusses the following main issues: the doctrine of the Trinity, the Messiah in the history of salvation, the doctrine of the incarnation, and the mission of the apostles to preach the news of the coming of the Messiah, in the person of Jesus of Nazareth, to all nations. It closes with a long list of quotations from the books of the prophets that the author interprets as biblical testimonies to the works and teachings of the Messiah manifest in the life and ministry of Jesus. Near the beginning of the treatise, as he begins the discussion of the doctrine of the Trinity, the author makes a statement of purpose in which the reader will readily recognize the intention to respond to the Qur'ān's critique of Christian doctrine. He writes,

> We praise you, O God, and we adore you and we glorify you in your creative Word and your holy, life-giving Spirit, one God, and one Lord, and one Creator. We do not separate God from his Word and his Spirit. God showed his power and his light in the Law and the Prophets, and the Psalms and the Gospel, that God and his Word and his Spirit are one God and one Lord. We will show this, if God will, in these revealed scriptures, to anyone who wants insight, [who] understands things, recognizes the truth and opens his breast to believe in God and His scriptures.[25]

One notices that the biblical books named in this passage are the very ones that are named in the Qur'ān, and what is more, what the author says about God, his Word, and his Spirit clearly echoes the passage quoted above from the Qur'ān, IV *an-Nisā* 171. But what is truly remarkable is that as the text goes on, the anonymous author includes as proof-texts, passages from the Qur'ān among the scriptures from which he quotes in testimony to the credibility of the doctrine of the Trinity. At one point, as he quotes passages from the scriptures that feature the one God speaking in the first person plural, he includes clear quotations from the Qur'ān. He says:

> You will find it also in the Qur'ān that "We created man in misery (XC:4), and We have opened the gates of heaven with water pouring down (LIV:11), and have said, and now you come unto us alone, as We created you at first (VI:94)." It said also, "Believe in God, and in his Word; and also in the Holy Spirit (IV:171)," but the Holy Spirit has brought it down "a mercy and a guidance from thy Lord (XVI:64, 102)." But why should I prove it from this and

Christlich-muslimische Gespräche im Mittelalter, ed. Martin Tamcke, Beiruter Texte und Studien 117 (Beirut: Ergon Verlag Würzburg in Kommission, 2007) 113–34..

25. Somewhat adapted and altered from Gibson, *Arabic Version*, 3 (English), 75 (Arabic).

> enlighten [you] when we find in the Law, and the Prophets and the Psalms and the Gospel, and you find in the Qur'ān that God and his Word and his Spirit are one God and one Lord? You have said that you believe in God and his Word and the Holy Spirit, so do not reproach us, O men, that we believe in God and his Word and his Spirit: and we worship God in his Word, and his Spirit, one God and one Lord and one Creator.[26]

In addition to the quotations from the Qur'ān in this passage, it is clear from other parts of the text that the author is thoroughly familiar with the Islamic scripture; indeed at the beginning of his work he even models the language of his introductory paragraphs on the Qur'ān's very distinctive modes of discourse, including echoes and repetitions of its Arabic diction.[27] So the question arises, does he consider the Qur'ān a revealed scripture on a par with the Law, the Prophets, the Psalms, and the Gospel? While the answer to this question is surely, "No," given the fact that throughout the treatise arguments from the Bible and Christian tradition are adduced expressly to respond to the challenge of Islamic teaching. Nevertheless, the author obviously thought that his quotations from the Qur'ān would have probative value for his apologetic purposes. For the rest, he achieves his aims largely by quoting liberally from the Bible, especially from the books of the Old Testament. He comments on these passages in such a way as to argue that they find their full meaning, and their fulfillment, in what one learns from the Gospel about the triune God and the incarnation of the Word of God. And this apologetic method would continue to be used by Christian apologists writing in Arabic throughout the whole period of our discussion. They very often intertwined testimonies from the scriptures with the other apologetic approaches they adopted to commend the credibility of Christian doctrines, and sometimes they even included long *catenae* of quotations from the Old and New Testaments, with exegetical commentary designed to meet the new challenges.[28]

26. Gibson, *Arabic Version*, 5–6 (English), 77–78 (Arabic). Note the identification of phrases from the Qur'ān.

27. See Mark N. Swanson, "Beyond Proof-Texting: Approaches to the Qur'ān in Some Early Arabic Christian Apologies," *The Muslim World* 88 (1998) esp. 305–8.

28. See Sidney H. Griffith, "Arguing from Scripture: The Bible in the Christian/Muslim Encounter in the Middle Ages," in *Scripture and Pluralism: Reading the Bible in the Religiously Plural Worlds of the Middle Ages and Renaissance*, ed. T. J. Heffernan and T. E. Burman, Studies in the History of Christian Traditions 123 (Leiden: Brill, 2006) 29–58.

B. *'Ilm al-Kalām*

Christian theoretical apologetics and polemics in Arabic developed almost in tandem with the evolution of Islamic theology, and while the degree of mutual conditioning and reactive influences is a matter of some discussion, the temporal and thematic coincidences are very noticeable.[29] It is generally agreed that the distinctive mode of Islamic systematic theology, the *'ilm al-Kalām*,[30] grew up with the Mu'tazilite school of thought, responding to developments in theoretical Arabic grammar and including elements of formal, largely Aristotelian logic provided by the contemporary translation movement. The Mu'tazilites flourished from the eighth century through the mid-ninth century, after which their school was eclipsed in official circles by the so-called Asharite, Maturidite, and Hanbalite movements, most of whose *'ulamā'*, or learned men, nevertheless carried on with the traditional theological method of the *'ilm al-kalām*.[31] The first generation of Christian *mutakallimūn* were contemporaries of the early Mu'tazilite *mutakallimūn* and the Christians composed their own *Kalām* treatises much on the model of and often in the idiom of their Muslim counterparts, in an effort the more convincingly in their milieu to purchase a modicum of credibility for their own doctrines and to suggest the inadequacy of the current Islamic systems of thought.[32] Nowhere is this method more in evidence than in the discussion of the doctrine of the Trinity.

Around the middle of the ninth century, a now unknown "Melkite" theologian who compiled a virtual *Summa Theologiae* for Christians in Arabic,[33] framed the theological and apologetic problem facing the

29. See, e.g., John Wansbrough, *The Sectarian Milieu: Content and Composition of Islamic Salvation History* (Oxford: Oxford University Press, 1978).

30. See Richard M. Frank, "The Science of Kalām," *Arabic Science and Philosophy* 2 (1992) 9–37.

31. See Robert Caspar, *Traité de théologie musulmane*, vol. 1, *Histoire de la pensée religieuse musulmane*, Collection "Studi arabo-islamici del PISAI" 1 (Rome: PISAI, 1987) 145–257. See also W. Montgomery Watt, *The Formative Period of Islamic Thought* (Edinburgh: Edingurgh University Press, 1973; repr., Oxford: One World, 1998).

32. See Griffith, *Church in the Shadow*, esp. 45–106.

33. On this very interesting and still unpublished text, see Khalil Samir, "La 'Somme des aspects de la foi,' oeuvre d'Abū Qurrah?" and Sidney H. Griffith, "A Ninth-Century *Summa Theologiae Arabica*," in *Actes du deuxième congrès international d'études arabes chrétiennes*, ed. Khalil Samir, Orientalia Christiana Analecta 226 (Rome: Pontifical Institute for Oriental Studies, 1986) 93–121 and 123–41. See also Sidney H. Griffith, "Islam and the Summa Theologiae Arabica; *Rabī'* I, 264 A.H.," *Jerusalem Studies in Arabic and*

Christians about the doctrine of the Trinity in the Islamic milieu as follows. After calling attention to the fact that in the past Christians had not neglected any way in which they might lead people to "belief in the one-ness of God and in the trinity of His one-ness [*imān biwaḥdāniyyati Allāh wa bitathlīth waḥdāniyyatihi*], and in His incarnation,"[34] and remarking that the earlier Christians had even been willing to argue with any adversary for the sake of the truth of the matter, the author now avers that in the past, the adversaries' language in their descriptions of God had been "a relentlessly horrid language."[35] By contrast, he says, the present situation is very different. He describes it as follows:

> The language of this [Muslim] community about God is a clear language, which ordinary people understand. I mean their saying, "There is no god but God." And there is no god but God, by which, however, they mean a god other than the Father, and the Son, and the Holy Spirit. From what they say, God does not generate, nor is He generated;[36] nor from what they say is there a Holy Spirit, save as a creature among creatures.[37] So their saying, "There is no god but God," and our saying it, is one in words but it differs in meaning. That is because we, the Christian community, when we say, "There is no god but God," we mean by it a living God, possessed of a living Spirit, which both causes to live and causes to die,[38] a mind, which determines everything He wills, and a Word, by means of which all being comes to be. What has no spirit, no mind and no word, is not alive, nor is a spirit that is added to [God], as they maintain, of His nature; it is rather a creature among creatures.[39]

The concern registered here about the Muslim community's clear "language [*kalām*] about God," which is the Arabic language of the Qur'ān and of the early Muslim *mutakallimūn*, recalls the fact that early Islamic

---

Islam 13 (1990) 225–64.

34. British Museum Oriental MS 4950, f. 5r.

35. Ibid., f. 5v.

36. The reference is to CXII *al-Ikhlāṣ* 3.

37. The allusion is to IV *an-Nisā* 171, and to other passages. See Griffith, "Holy Spirit," in McAuliffe, *Encyclopaedia of the Qur'ān*, 2:442–44.

38. The Qur'ān says, "It is God who causes to live and causes to die." III *Āl 'Imrān* 156; "God's is the dominion over heaven and earth. There is no god but He; He causes to live and causes to die." VII *al-A'rāf* 158 and IX *at-Tawbah* 116.

39. British Museum Oriental MS 4950, f. 5v.

systematic theology (*'ilm al-kalām*) was driven by current developments in theoretical Arabic grammar. And nowhere was this more in evidence than in the controversies that embroiled the Mu'tazilites of Baṣrah and Baghdad in the first half of the ninth century about the proper ways to understand and speak about the divine attributes (*ṣifāt Allāh*), the "beautiful names [*al-asmā' al-ḥusnah*] of God," as they were called, culled from the Qur'ān.[40] It seemed to the Mu'tazilites that, if taken literally, the divine attributes, in addition to the dangers of implying anthropomorphism, would, by the rules of Arabic grammar, also postulate the existence in God's being of corresponding, eternal acts or facts that would in turn compromise God's absolute oneness. For example, to affirm that God is one who sees or hears, as the Qur'ān says, would on the current grammatical understanding, if taken literally, require that eternal acts of seeing and hearing be attributed to God's eternal being or essence.[41] Accordingly, most Mu'tazilites maintained that the divine attributes must be understood metaphorically, while some thinkers devised formulae they thought would avoid the unacceptable conclusions. The earliest Christian *mutakallimūn* in the Islamic milieu saw an opportunity in this controversy among Muslims to make use of the givens of the discussion to defend the credibility of the Christian doctrine of the Trinity, implying in the process that the Christian doctrine even offered a solution to the conceptual problems faced by the Muslim *mutakallimūn*.

The first of the Christian thinkers seriously to take advantage of the intellectual developments in the Islamic community for the sake of a more effective Christian apologetic seems to have been Patriarch Timothy I (r. 780–823), of the so-called Nestorian Church of the East. He moved his see from its original home in Seleucia-Ctesiphon to Baghdad, where he enjoyed entrée to the caliph's court and its attendant scholarly circles. In a

40. See Richard M. Frank, *Beings and Their Attributes: The Teaching of the Basrian School of the Mu'tazila in the Classical Period* (Albany: State University of New York Press, 1978); Daniel Gimaret, *Les noms divins en Islam: Exégèse lexicographique et théologique* (Paris: Cerf, 1988).

41. For example, the Baṣrain Muslim *mutakallim* Abū Muḥammad 'Abdallāh ibn Muḥammad ibn Kullāb (d. 855) is on record as having affirmed that "'the meaning of the statement "God is knowing" is that an act of knowing belongs to Him'; that is to say, there is subsistent in Him an act of knowing by virtue of which He is said to be knowing." Frank, *Beings and Their Attributes*, 12, and see also 28, n.7. For more on Ibn Kullāb, see Josef van Ess, *Theologie und Gesellschaft im 2. und 3. Jahrhundert Hidschra: Eine Geschichte des religiösen Denkens im frühen Islam*, 6 vols. (Berlin: de Gruyter, 1991–1997) 4:180–94. Most Mu'tazilites rejected Kibn Kullāb's teaching about the divine attributes on the grounds that like Christian Trinitarian theology, it admitted the existence of eternal entities in God. See Van Ess, *Theologie und Gesellschaft*, 4:188.

number of long letters, written in Syriac, the patriarch gives details of his encounters and conversations with Muslim thinkers as well as responses to Christian correspondents who posed questions about how to answer Muslim queries.[42] Needless to say, the doctrines of the Trinity and the incarnation received most of the attention, and Patriarch Timothy seems also to have been the first Christian to tell of his conversation with a Muslim *mutakallim* about God, including the method of using the occasion of the current conversations about the divine attributes among Muslims to commend the credibility of the doctrine of the Trinity.[43] Subsequently, the earliest theologians regularly to write in Arabic from all three Christian churches followed suit: the "Melkite" Theodore Abū Qurrah (c. 755–c. 830),[44] the "Jacobite" Ḥabīb ibn Khidmah Abū Rā'iṭah (d.c. 851),[45] and the "Nestorian" 'Ammār al-Baṣrī (*fl.* before 850).[46] Here we shall focus our attention on the latter, whose interaction with Muslim *mutakallimūn* seems most obvious and whose work on Trinitarian theology has been the least studied by modern scholars.[47]

As is evident from his name, 'Ammār al-Baṣrī came from the very city that in the first half of the ninth century was one of the most important

42. See Sidney H. Griffith, "The Syriac Letters of Patriarch Timothy I and the Birth of Christian *Kalām* in the Mu'tazilite Milieu of Baghdad and Baṣrah in Early Islamic Times," in *Syriac Polemics: Studies in Honour of Gerrit Jan Reinink*, ed. Wout Jac. Van Bekkum et al., Orientalia Lovaniensia Analecta 170 (Leuven: Uitgeverij Petters en Departement of Oosterse Studies, 2007) 103–32.

43. See Thomas Hurst, "Letter 40 of the Nestorian Patriarch Timothy I (727–823): An Edition and Translation," master's thesis (Catholic University of America, 1981); Hanna Cheikho, *Dialectique du langage sur Dieu de Timothée I (728–823) à Serge* (Rome: Pontifical Institute for Oriental Studies, 1983).

44. See John Lamoreaux (trans.), *Theodore Abū Qurrah*, Library of the Christian East 1 (Provo, UT: Brigham Young University Press, 2005).

45. See Sandra Toenies Keating, *Defending the "People of Truth" in the Early Islamic Period: The Christian Apologies of Abū Rā'i˜ah*, History of Muslim-Christian Relations 4 (Leiden: Brill, 2006).

46. See Michel Hayek, "'Ammār al-Baṣrī: La première Somme de Théologie Chrétienne en Langue Arabe, ou Deux Apologies du Christianisme," *Islamochristiana* 2 (1976) 69–113; Sidney H. Griffith, "Ammār al-Baṣrī's *Kitāb al-burhān*: Christian *Kalām* in the First Abbasid Century," *Le Muséon* 96 (1983) 145–81.

47. See the earlier study by Sidney H. Griffith, "The Concept of *al-uqnūm* in 'Ammār al-Baṣrī's Apology for the Doctrine of the Trinity," in *Actes du premier congrès international d'études arabes chrétiennes (Goslar, septembre 1980)*, ed. Khalil Samir, Orientalia Christiana Analecta 218 (Rome: Pontifical Institute for Oriental Studies, 1982) 169–91.

centers of the then burgeoning Islamic sciences.[48] While not much is known of his biography, two important works of Christian theology in Arabic from his pen have come down to us, the *Kitāb al-burhān* and the *Kitāb masā'il wa l-ajwibah*, neither of which has been translated into a Western language.[49] But an interesting thing about the work of 'Ammār is that at least one important Mu'tazilite *mutakallim*, his fellow Baṣrian Abū Hudhayl al-'Allāf (d. c. 841/845), seems to have been familiar with his teaching; Ibn an-Nadīm reports in his *Fihrist* that Abū Hudhayl wrote a book titled, *Kitāb 'alā 'Ammār an-Naṣrānī fī radd 'alā n-naṣārā*, or "Against 'Ammār the Christian, in Refutation of the Christians."[50] And perhaps more to the point, Abū Hudhayl, who was arguably one of the most important of the early Mu'tazilites,[51] was much concerned with the proper way to understand the divine attributes. It was he, for example, who developed the formula according to which the act or fact bespoken by a given divine attribute should simply be said to be God. For example, according to Abū Hudhayl, to say that God is "knowing" (*'ālim*) is to affirm that "He is knowing by an act of knowledge [*'ilm*] that is He," and vice versa, that is, according to this attribution, God is knowledge.[52]

'Ammār al-Baṣrī approached his defense of the doctrine of the Trinity against the background of just such a Muslim concern for the ontological

48. See Charles Pellat, *Le milieu basrien et la formation de Jāḥiz* (Paris: Librairie d'Amérique et d'Orient Adrien-Maisonneuve, 1953).

49. The Arabic edition has been published by Michel Hayek, *'Ammār al-Baṣrī: apologie et controverses* (Beirut: Dar el-Machreq, 1977). For a summary of what is known about 'Ammār, and for the tables of contents of his two extant treatises, see Bénédicte Landron, *Chrétiens et musulmans en Irak: Attitudes Nestoriennes vis-à-vis de l'Islam*, Études Chrétiennes Arabes (Paris: Cariscript, 1994) 60–66. It is worth noting in the present context that 'Ammār, like the Muslim *mutakallimūn* in his Baṣrian milieu, dedicated his *Kitāb masā'il wa l-ajwibah* to the reigning caliph, unfortunately without naming him. See the discussion in Griffith, "'Ammār al-Baṣrī's *Kitāb al-burhān*," 150–52.

50. See J. W. Fück, "Some Hitherto Unpublished Texts on the Mu'tazilite Movement from Ibn al-Nadim's Kitāb al-Fihrist," in *Professor Muhamad Shafi Presentation Volume*, ed. S. M. Abdullah (Lahore, Pakistan: Punjab University Press, 1955) 62; Bayard Dodge, (ed. and trans.), *The Fihrist of al-Nadīm: A Tenth Century Survey of Muslim Culture*, 2 vols. (New York: Columbia University Press, 1970) 1:394.

51. On Abū Hudhayl and his significance, see now Van Ess, *Theologie und Gesellschaft*, 3:209–91. In all likelihood, Abū Hudhayl developed his distinctive teaching about the divine attributes in reaction to positions like the one espoused by Ibn Kullāb. See n. 41 above.

52. Ibid., 3:274. See also Richard M. Frank, "The Divine Attributes according to the Teaching of Abū Hudhayl al-'Allāf," *Le Muséon* 82 (1969) 451–506.

implications of the divine attributes. First, he attempts to reduce to absurdity the Muʿtazilite doctrine, and specifically the teaching espoused by Abū Hudhayl. And then he argues that Christian Trinitarian theology is actually the way out of the logical dilemma that the Muslim *mutakallimūn* faced. In the *Kitāb masāʾil wa l-ajwibah*, ʿAmmār approaches the topic as follows:

> Let us ask them about "the one" [*al-wāḥid*] that is so light on their tongues . . . so that they might clarify what they believe on faith about Him—in the face of their divergence from the outward sense of their own words, and their transformation of the Creator, whom they say is "living" [*ḥayy*] and "speaking" [*nāṭiq*], into an inanimate being having no life [*ḥayyah*], and no word [*kalimah*].[53]

ʿAmmār then puts this rhetorical question to his Muslim adversary: "How, according to you, is the name [*ism*], 'the living one' [*al-ḥayy*], derived?" And he immediately gives the answer, "The name, 'the living one,' is derived only from life [*al-ḥayyah*]. . . . For we know the thing [*ash-shay*'] that is named only by what it has. And it is not named by what it does not have."[54] With this question and answer, ʿAmmār puts his finger on precisely the Arabic grammatical presupposition that caused a problem for the Muslim *mutakallimūn*. The assumption was that verbal adjectives (*ṣifāt*), such as the divine attributes, are derived from nouns, and nouns by their very nature, according to the current theory, indicate acts or facts, entities.[55] According to this logic, to say that God is "living" is to say that there is a reality, "life," somehow existent in God as the real meaning or "referent" (*al-maʿnā*) of the predicative adjective "living" in the statement "God is living." So, to avoid the implication, unacceptable to Muslims, that to say "God is living" means that God has life, Abū Hudhayl affirmed that the predication of the attribute "living" of God means that God "is living by a life that is He," to quote the report in Abū al-Ḥasan al-Ashʿarī's (873–935) recapitulation of the teachings of the Muʿtazilites.[56]

ʿAmmār al-Baṣrī's reaction to this line of thinking is evident in his statement, "Whatever does not necessarily have life, either essential or accidental, necessarily has death, since beyond doubt death is the opposite of

53. Hayek, *Apologie et controverses*, 46.

54. Ibid., 47.

55. See Frank, *Beings and Their Attributes*, 12–14, and esp. 28, n.8.

56. H. Ritter, *Die dogmatischen Lehren der Anhänger des Islam von Abū al-Hasan ʿAlī ibn ʿIsmāʿil al-Ashʿarī*, 2 vols. (Istanbul: Devlet Matbaasi, 1929–1930) 1:165.

life."[57] And he proceeds to apply the same sort of reasoning to other Qur'ānic descriptive adjectives that describe God such as "seeing" (*baṣīr*), "hearing" (*samīʿ*), "speaking" (*nāṭiq*), and the rest. He points out that, according to the prevailing grammatical logic employed by the *mutakallimūn*, when these attributes are predicated of God, in Arabic usage they inevitably bespeak the act or fact of "sight" (*baṣar*), "hearing" (*samʿ*), "speaking" (*kalimah*) [*sic*] as referents in God; God must somehow have them. And ʿAmmār argues that the Christian doctrine of the Trinity actually supplies the only logical provision for what the grammatical logic of the Arabic language requires in the matter of the proper understanding of the divine attributes. Furthermore, as he goes along he shows both the unacceptable consequences of adopting a solution like the one attributed to Abū Hudhayl, and he rebuts the charges of tritheism and "associationism" (*ash-shirk*) that the Muslim *mutakallimūn* customarily brought against the Christians and their doctrine of the Trinity.

In reference to a typical Muslim adversary, who would say to a Christian that the doctrine of the Trinity amounts to tritheism, ʿAmmār says,

> Since he has fled from affirming the Word and the Spirit so that he should not be required to acknowledge three referents [*tathlīth al-maʿānī*] in the essence of the Creator, and thereby, according to him, nullify *at-tawḥīd*, he has fallen into the denial of the Creator and he has made Him dead, having no life and no word. . . . While in all His scriptures, He describes Himself as having a Spirit and a Word.[58]

From here ʿAmmār goes on to state the Christian claim. He says,

> Before God we are blameless of alleging three gods. Rather, by our saying Father, Son and Holy Spirit, we want no more than to substantiate the statement that God is living [*ḥayy*], and speaking [*nāṭiq*]. And the Father is the one whom we consider to have life [*ḥayyah*] and word [*kalimah*]. The life is the Holy Spirit, and the word is the Son. It is not like what those who differ with us ascribe to us, namely that we fashion a female companion for God, and a son from her.[59]

In the last sentence one recognizes an allusion to a passage in the Qur'ān (LXXII *al-Jinn* 3) that Muslim polemicists sometimes quoted in

57. Hayek, *Apologie et controverses*, 47.
58. Ibid., 48.
59. Ibid., 48–49.

reference to what they alleged would be the implication of confessing Jesus, the Messiah, Mary's son, to be the Son of God.

ʿAmmār al-Baṣrī develops his apology for the credibility of the Christian doctrine of the Trinity by making the claim that of all the attributes of God that are found in the Bible or in the Qur'ān, only two of them—namely, the attributes "living" (*ḥayy*) and "speaking" (*nāṭiq*)—designate referents/meanings (*maʿānī*), namely "life" (*ḥayyah*) and "word" (*kalimah*), that are, as ʿAmmār says, "of the ground of the 'essence' [*dhāt*], and of the constitution of the very being or substance [*jawhar*]"[60] to which they are attributed. For, as ʿAmmār goes on to say, "life" is the attributed reality that makes the difference between the animate and the inanimate, and "speech" is the attributed reality that makes the difference between the rational and the irrational. No other attributes of essence or action, such as "seeing" and "hearing," are basic, constitutive attributes of the beings to which they are attributed, and no one of them designates a grade or state (*ḥāl*) of being by reason of its occurrence. Rather, the occurrence of any other attribute, such as any one of those among God's "noble names,"[61] as ʿAmmār calls the divine attributes, necessarily presumes the prior occurrence of the essential constitutive attributes of His being, that is, "life" and "word," as the condition of its own true attribution. Because "life" and "speech" are therefore the essential constitutive attributes of being, which differentiate the animate from the inanimate and the rational from the irrational, after reviewing how all the other scriptural attributes of God actually presume the prior existence of these two, ʿAmmār says,

> So therefore, we affirm "life" and "speech," apart from anything else we have mentioned, to be in the substantial essence of the Creator, since we find the two of them to be of the constitution of the [divine] being/substance [*jawhar*]. He has himself ascribed them to himself and He has corroborated the testimonies to them in his scriptures.[62]

As a matter of fact, ʿAmmār argues, the other divine attributes, especially the ones mentioned in the Qur'ān and the ones most often discussed by the Muslim *mutakallimūn*, such as "seeing," "hearing," "powerful," "merciful," "knowing," etc., all presume the priority of "living" and "speaking" as basic differentials of "being" that allow for the predication of all

60. Ibid., 52.
61. Ibid., 54.
62. Ibid., 53.

the other attributes. Therefore, none of the divine attributes except "living" and "speaking" actually bespeak acts or facts that are constitutive of being. Rather, the other attributes ascribe adventitious, even accidental acts or facts to the divine being. And it is on this basis of this logic that 'Ammār is then prepared to object to an Islamic formula such as the one that Abū Hudhayl elaborated for understanding the ontological status of the divine attributes, namely, that God is, for example, "knowing" (*'ālim*) by an "act of knowledge" (*'ilm*) that is He. For such a formula, which fails adequately to distinguish between the significant differences in ontological status affirmed by the several attributes, effectively reduces God's very being, instance by instance, to a series of lesser states of being, accidental and even material, all of which presume the priority and reality of the constitutive states of God's being, that is, his life and his word, for their own subsistence.

But what about the ontological status of the one God's two essential attributes, His Spirit and His Word, the Father's Son and His Spirit? 'Ammār explains that God's Word and His Spirit are understood by Christians to be two *qunūmayn* (sing. *qunūm*), and that "the one God" (*Allāhu al-wāḥid*) exists in three *aqānīm*, Father, Son/Word, and Spirit/Life. The enigmatic Arabic term *qunūm* (pl. *aqānīm*) that 'Ammār, like all other Arabic-speaking Christian theologians, uses in this connection is in Arabic a calque on the Syriac term *qnômâ* (pl. *qnômê*), which is usually translated as "self" in English. Syriac-speaking theologians regularly used this term in theological discourse to translate the philosophico-theological term *hypostasis*, as it was used by the Greek-speaking Fathers of the Church in Trinitarian and christological discourse. 'Ammār defines the term *al-qunūm* as follows: "For us, *al-qunūm* is a perfect thing/entity [*shay'*], not deficient and not needing anything other than itself for its subsistence [*thabāt*]."[63] In another place, 'Ammār says, "*Al-qunūm* is a Syriac word, as we have said, and its meaning is 'individual' [*al-'ayn*], something particular [*al-khāṣṣ*], something perfect [*al-kāmil*], independent in itself, rejecting from itself any need for anything else for the subsistence [*qiwām*] of its essence [*dhāt*]."[64] 'Ammār's definition is consistent with that normally given by his fellow East Syrian scholars.[65]

63. Ibid., 50.

64. Ibid., 162. Just previously, on the same page, 'Ammār had explained to his imagined Muslim interlocutor that he uses the Syriac word to name the three "particularities" (*khwaṣṣ*) in God because "there is not anything in your language [Arabic] you could use for a name."

65. See, for example, *Lexicon Syriacum auctore Hassano bar Bahlule*, ed. Rubens Duval, 3 vols. (Paris: E Typographeo Rei Publicae/Ernest Lerous, 1901) vol. 2, cols. 1804–6.

But he goes further to point out that in the place of the Greek philosophical term *hypostasis*, Syriac-speaking Christian people use the Syriac biblical term *qnômâ* in their expression of the traditional Trinitarian formula "after they found it mentioned in the Gospel."[66] And he specifies that it occurs in the Messiah's own saying, "Just as the Father has life in himself [*baqnômeh*], so has He granted the Son also to have life in himself [*baqnômeh*]" (John 5:26).[67]

Unlike most of the other Arabic-speaking Christian theologians of his own era and later,[68] ʿAmmār refused to attempt to translate or to paraphrase this difficult Syriac loanword into Arabic, utilizing some Arabic equivalent for "person" (*al-wajh*) or "individual" (*ash-shakhṣ*), as most Christian writers did,[69] on the grounds that in Arabic the denotations and connotations of all the available translation terms were misleading. For example, it was very common for Arabic-speaking theologians to adopt the Arabic term *ash-shakhṣ* (pl. *al-ashkhāṣ*) in the sense of "individual," to translate the technical term *hypostasis/qnômâ/uqnūm* into Arabic. ʿAmmār, after having provided the appropriate definition, preferred simply to speak in Arabic of the three *aqānīm* of the one God. He said:

> We have not named them [i.e., the *aqānīm*] three *ashkhāṣ*, so do not let anyone imagine that we have named them *ashkhāṣ*, because for us *ash-shakhṣ* is a corporeal body [*jism*], defined by its dimensions and members that mark it out among other corporeal bodies.[70]

ʿAmmār al-Baṣrī argued on the basis of what he presented as the proper understanding of the divine attributes, according to the rules of the

66. Hayek, *Apologie et controverses*, 52 and 163.

67. See ibid., 163. It was perhaps St. Ephraem the Syrian (c. 306–372) who had initiated this usage just about five hundred years before the time of ʿAmmār. See Sidney H. Griffith, "Faith Seeking Understanding in the Thought of St. Ephraem the Syrian," in *Faith Seeking Understanding: Learning and the Catholic Tradition*, ed. George C. Berthold (Manchester, NH: St. Anselm College Press, 1991) 35–55.

68. The translation of the traditional, mostly Greek, technical terms of Christian theology was a constant problem for Arabic-speaking theologians, and among them they used a number of different, usually unsatisfactory, Arabic equivalents for these terms. See also Haddad, *La trinité divine*, and Khoury, *Matériaux*, 2:305–28.

69. See Bo Holmberg, "'Person' in the Trinitarian Doctrine of Christian Arabic Apologetics and Its Background in the Syriac Church Fathers," in *Studia Patristica* 25, ed. Elizabeth A. Livingstone (Leuven: Peeters, 1993) 300–307.

70. Hayek, *Apologie et controverses*, 162.

current theoretical Arabic grammar as interpreted by the *mutakallimūn*, that logically one must describe God as alive and rational, having "life" and "word" as essentially constitutive of his being.[71] He argued further that the one God, in virtue of the essential particularities of his divine being, therefore exists in three *aqānīm*. ʿAmmār thought that he had reasonably shown on this basis that trebling (*tathlīth*) the referents (*al-maʿānī*) of those attributes that are constitutive of the divine essence does not falsify the affirmation of the oneness of God (*at-tawḥīd*) but supports it and effectively escapes the dilemma faced by the Muslims. As for the theoretical problem of the one and the many, and the real meaning of "one," ʿAmmār was content with repeating the traditional analogies Christian apologists for the doctrine of the Trinity had long used.[72] But the philosophers were not so easily convinced.

C. Philosophical Logic

The earliest Arabic-speaking philosophers in the Islamic world, who were for the most part dependent on translations of Greek philosophical and logical texts originally made by Christians from Syriac into Arabic,[73] were concerned, like their Christian counterparts, to explore the philosophical dimensions of *at-tawḥīd*, confessing that God is one. It is significant in this connection that the discussion of "oneness" (*waḥdāniyyah*) and its philosophical implications, against the background of Greek logic and metaphysics, was high on the list of the major concerns of the first two philosophers in this milieu whose names are still widely known, Abū Yūsuf Yaʿqūb ibn Isḥāq al-Kindī (c. 801–866), known as the "philosopher of the Arabs," and Abū Naṣr al-Fārābī (c. 870–950), known as the "second master," that is, after Aristotle. Al-Kindī, for whom "philosophy was to vindicate the pursuit of rational activity as an activity in the service of Islam,"[74] spoke at

71. Other Christian apologists writing in Arabic followed much the same method, sometimes choosing other attributes as constitutive of the divine essence. See Haddad, *La trinité divin*, esp. 232–33; Khoury, *Matériaux*, 4:47–90.

72. See the list of the most common analogies in Khoury, *Matéteriaux*, 4:286–305, 435–78.

73. See Henri Hugonnard-Roche, *La logique d'Aristote du grec au syriaque: Études sur la transmission des texts de l'Organon et leur interpretation philosophique*, Textes et Traditions 9 (Paris: Librairie Philosophique J. Vrin, 2004); Gutas, *Greek Thought, Arabic Culture.*

74. Gerhard Endress, "The Circle of al-Kindī: Early Arabic Translations from the

some length in his treatise *On First Philosophy* about divine existence and oneness.[75] And he also wrote a treatise specifically dedicated to laying out his logical objections to the Christian doctrine of the Trinity, a text that survives only in the quotations from it provided by the Christian philosopher Yaḥyā ibn ʿAdī (893–974) in his refutation of al-Kindī's objections.[76]

Al-Fārābī is on everyone's list of world-class philosophers, and in the context of our present concern it is noteworthy that among his teachers were two Christians: the virtually unknown Yūḥannā ibn Óaylān (d. between 908 and 932) and the well-known Abū Bishr Mattā ibn Yūnus (d. 940). Al-Fārābī's student, and his successor as the head of the so-called Baghdad Peripatetics, was the aforementioned "Jacobite" Christian apologist and logician Yaḥyā ibn ʿAdī. He in turn became the center of a circle of philosophers, Christian and Muslim, whose work was very much under the influence of al-Fārābī, so much so that one modern scholar speaks of the "Age of Farabism, 870–1023,"[77] an era that is virtually coincident with the flourishing of Christian theology in Arabic. Not surprisingly, as a confessing Muslim philosopher, al-Fārābī, like all the Muslim thinkers of his era, was much interested in the philosophical implications of *at-tawḥīd*, and in fact, drawing on his deep knowledge of the Alexandrian philosophical tradition, he wrote a book titled in English by its modern editor, *On One*

Greek and the Rise of Islamic Philosophy," in *The Ancient Tradition in Christian and Islamic Hellenism: Studies on the Transmission of Greek Philosophy and Sciences*, ed. G. Endress and R. Kruk (Leiden: Research School CNWS, School of Asian, African, and Amerindian Studies, 1997) 50.

75. See Michael E. Marmura and John Rist, "Al-Kindī's Discussion of Divine Existence and Oneness," in *Probing in Islamic Philosophy: Studies in the Philosophies of Ibn Sina, al-Ghazali and Other Major Muslim Thinkers*, ed. Michael E. Marmura (Binghamton, NY: Global Academic, State University of New York at Binghamton, 2005) 337–53; Peter Adamson, "Al-Kindī and the Muʿtazila: Divine Attributes, Creation and Freedom," *Arabic Sciences and Philosophy* 13 (2003) 45–77.

76. The text was first published by Augustin Périer, "Un traité de Yahyâ ben ʿAdî: Défense du dogme de la trinité contre les objections d'al-Kindî; texte arabe publié pour la première fois et traduit," *Revue de l'Orient Chrétien*, 3rd series, vol. 2 (22) (1920–1921) 3–21. Al-Kindī's text, extracted from Yaḥyā ibn ʿAdī's treatise, is published independently, with discussion and a new French translation, in *Oeuvres philosophiques et scientifiques d'al-Kindī*, vol. 2, *Métaphysique et Cosmologie*, ed. Roshdi Rashed and Jean Jolivet, Islamic Philosophy, Theology and Science, Texts and Studies 29 (Leiden: Brill, 1998) 119–28.

77. See Ian Richard Netton, *Al-Fārābī and His School* (Richmond, UK: Curzon, 1992). For much more on Yaḥyā ibn ʿAdī and his circle of "Baghdad Peripatetics," see also Joel L. Kraemer, *Humanism in the Renaissance of Islam: The Cultural Revival during the Buyid Age* (Leiden: Brill 1986).

and Unity,[78] in which al-Fārābī discusses what one means when he says that something is "one" (*wāḥid*). This book seems very much to have been in the background, as we shall see below, of a book on the same subject by his Christian student Yaḥyā ibn ʿAdī.

Yaḥyā ibn ʿAdī was both a logician in the Aristotelian tradition and a Christian apologist, both in defense of his own "Jacobite" Christian faith against the objections of other Christians and in defense of the basic articles of the Christian creed against the objections of Muslims.[79] Indeed, in his great book *Guide of the Perplexed*, Maimonides spoke of Yaḥyā as a *mutakallim* and said that Yaḥyā was one of those from whom the Muslim *mutakallimūn* learned the arts of the *ʿilm al-kalām*.[80] While being thus put into the company of the *mutakallimūn* would have appalled Yaḥyā the philosopher, the fact is that he was an able apologist. In defense of the doctrine of the Trinity, Yaḥyā wrote a number of shorter essays on various aspects of the subject;[81] and, as mentioned above, he also wrote a rebuttal of the philosopher al-Kindī's objections to the Christian doctrine,[82] as well as a rebuttal against the Muslim thinker Abū ʿĪṣā al-Warrāq's attack *Against the Trinity*.[83] Perhaps most importantly, Yaḥyā wrote his own monograph, *Kitāb fī t-tawḥīd*,[84] in order very systematically and positively to set out his reasoning in defense of the doctrine of the one and three.

At the outset, it is important to recognize the fact that Yaḥyā wrote a generation and more after the time of ʿAmmār al-Baṣrī and the first

78. Abū Naṣr al-Fārābī, *Kitāb al-wāḥid wa l-waḥdah*, ed. Muhsin Mahdi (Casablanca: Toubkal, 1989).

79. See Augustin Périer, *Yaḥyā ben ʿAdī: Un philosophe arabe Chrétien du Xe siècle* (Paris: Gabalda & Geuthner, 1920); Gerhard Endress, *The Works of Yaḥyā ibn ʿAdī: An Analytical Inventory* (Wiesbaden: Reichert, 1977); Emilio Platti, *La grande polémique antinestorienne de Yaḥyā B. ʿAdī*, CSCO 427 & 428 (Louvain: Peeters, 1981); Emilio Platti, *Yaḥyā ibn ʿAdī: Théologien Chrétien et philosophe arabe; sa théologie de l'incarnation*, Orientalia Lovaniensia Analecta 14 (Leuven: Katholieke Universiteit Leuven, Departement Orientalistick, 1983).

80. See Maimonides, *The Guide of the Perplexed*, trans. Shlomo Pines (Chicago: University of Chicago Press, 1963) 1:177–78.

81. Augustin Périer, *Petits traits apologétiques de Yahyâ ben ʿAdî: Texte arabe, édié pour la première fois d'après les manuscripts de Paris, de Rome et de Munich, et traduit en français* (Paris: Gabalda & Geuthner, 1920) 11–68.

82. See n. 75 above.

83. See Thomas, *Anti-Christian Polemic in Early Islam*.

84. Khalil Samir, *Le traité de l'unité de Yaḥyā ibn ʿAdī (893–974): Étude et édition critique*, Patrimoine Arabe Chrétien 2 (Rome: Librairie Saint-Paul & Pontificio Istituto Orientale, 1980).

generation of Christian *mutakallimūn*, who had already set the agenda for Trinitarian theology in Arabic, specifically in terms of their developing their own reasoning in the idiom of and on the pattern of reasoning employed in the Muʿtazilite *kalām* about the divine attributes. We saw an example of this in the works of ʿAmmār. Yaḥyā inherited and further developed this approach to the subject, via the discussion about the ontological status of the attributes, but he couched his own discourse not so much in the idiom of the *mutakallimūn* as in the Greek philosophical and logical terms of his own discipline.

The philosopher al-Kindī had said that he would challenge the Christians for the unreasonableness of their *at-tathlīth* on the basis of "logic and philosophy," and, more specifically, on the grounds that their Trinitarian confession necessarily involved the repulsive idea of introducing "composition" (*at-tarkīb*) into the Godhead. He said the following about the *aqānīm/hypostases* of the Christian Trinity, by which, he specified, "they mean 'individual persons' [*ashkhāṣ*]":

> It is necessarily the case that each one of them is a composite of the substance [*jawhar*] which comprises them and of the particular property [*khāṣṣah*] that particularizes it. Every composite is caused and nothing caused is eternal. Therefore, the Father is not eternal, nor is the Son eternal, nor is the Holy Spirit eternal. They are both eternal and not eternal; this is the ugliest absurdity.[85]

In his response to al-Kindī, whom he calls "the philosopher," Yaḥyā argues that given the Muslim philosopher's own description of God as simultaneously God (*ilāh*), as "one" (*wāḥid*), and as "substance" (*jawhar*), al-Kindī too faced a logical conundrum involving the notions of "one" and "three." In the sequel, Yaḥyā proceeds to find fault with al-Kindī's use of the categories defined in Porphyry's *Eisagoge* to discredit the Christian doctrine, arguing that the philosopher had misunderstood and misused the technical terms involved when it came to his discussion of the Christian doctrinal formulae, but he overlooked the same difficulties involved in his own affirmations regarding the one God. In the end, according to Yaḥyā, the matter came down to the proper understanding of what one means when he predicates "one" or "many" of a subject. And he explains that God is "one" in number in reference to his "substance"/"being" (*jawhar*), while in reference to his "quiddity" or "whatness" (*māhiyyah*), which, according to Yaḥyā, is essentially described as being "generous/good" (*jawwād*),

85. Périer, "Un traité," 4; Rashed and Jolivet, *Oeuvres Philosophiques*, 2:123.

"wise" (*ḥakīm*), and "powerful" (*qādir*), he is "three." For these predicates, Yaḥyā argues, bespeak actual "meanings" or essential "referents" (*ma'ānī*) in God, each one of which differs from the other two.[86] Yaḥyā follows much the same line of reasoning in his treatise on *at-tawḥīd*, in which he goes to considerable lengths to dispose of what he considers to be logically faulty definitions of "the one" (*al-wāḥid*), such as those usually employed by Muslim thinkers, and then he explains what he regards as the proper understanding of the predicate "one" (*wāḥid*) in reference to God: the Creator is one by definition, in reference to His being the subject of the predications of the divine attributes; He is three in reference to the three essential attributes (*ṣifāt*) of His being, "generosity," "wisdom," and "power," the existence of which are logically and ontologically prior to the predication of all other divine attributes.[87]

Having just previously considered 'Ammār al-Baṣrī's apology for the reasonableness of the Christian doctrine of the Trinity in response to the objections of Muslim *mutakallimūn* like Abū Hudhayl al-'Allāf, one will observe on the one hand a similar line of thought on Yaḥyā's part with regard to the assumptions made about the significance of the divine attributes and their referents, albeit that the essential three are different in Yaḥyā's account.[88] On the other hand, the whole discussion in both al-Kindī's and Yaḥyā's treatises is conducted within a completely different logical frame of reference, namely, that of Aristotle's *Organon* as presented in Porphyry's *Eisagoge*, as opposed to a logic based on the premises of theoretical Arabic grammar as deployed in the *'ilm al-kalām*, in 'Ammār's and Abū Hudhayl's works.

86. See Périer, *Un traité*, 12 and 13.

87. See Samir, *Le traité de l'unité*.

88. As was mentioned earlier, in the course of their apologies different Arabic-speaking theologians in fact spoke of different divine attributes as composing the triad of essential divine attributes, bespeaking the corresponding essential referents in the Godhead, the existence of which, they argued, is presumed for the predication of all other attributes. In his works on the Trinity, Yaḥyā ibn 'Adī himself uses two different triads; earlier, as in his refutation of al-Kindī, he speaks of the attributes "generosity," "wisdom," and "power"; later in his career, in other works, he uses the analogy or similitude of the tripartite process of reasoning, *'aql*, *'āqil*, and *ma'qūl*, i.e., "reason," "reasoning," and "reasoned." The different triads have different backgrounds in the several traditions, while the underlying logic of their deployment remains much the same. See the discussion in Haddad, *La trinité divine*, 218–33, and especially in Samir, *Le traité de l'unité*, xix–xx; 126–29 (Arabic). See also Emilio Platti, "La doctrine des chrétiens d'après Abū 'Īṣā al-Warrāq dans son traité sur la Trinité," *MIDEO* 20 (1991) esp. 17–22.

Preferring to base his arguments on Aristotelian logic, and often pointing out the logical fallacies in the arguments of his adversaries, Yaḥyā ibn ʿAdī seldom referred to the scriptures in his discussions of aspects of the doctrine of the Trinity, nor did he pay much attention to the analogies from nature that earlier Christian apologists employed so profusely. But there were exceptions. For example, in one place he refers very generally to the Old Testament, the New Testament, the Books of the Prophets, the Gospel (*al-injīl*), the Acts of the Apostles (*al-ḥawāriyyīn*), and the Epistles of the Apostles (*rasāʾil al-ḥawāriyyīn*), followed by mention of "the leaders/*imāms* [*al-aʾimmah*] and the scholars [*al-ʿulamāʾ*] like Dionysius, Gregory, Basil the Great, and John Chrysostom."[89] One notices the distinctly Islamic terms. In another place, Yaḥyā cites the testimony of the Gospel, without mentioning a specific passage, to explain why the verbal adjective "reasoning"/"understanding" (*ʿāqil*) refers to the "Son" in the triad *ʿaql, ʿāqil, maʿqūl*, rather than either one of the other two members of the analogy. He says,

> The Gospel mentions the fact that the Son is the incarnate one, and not the Father and the Spirit, so therefore it is necessary that the similitude for the Son be only *ʿāqil* ("one reasoning") rather than *maʿqūl* ("reasoned object"), and that is because it is possible for a human being to become a "reasoner."[90]

While Yaḥyā was thus sparing in his use of scripture and of analogies, in one of his short essays in defense of the reasonableness of the doctrine of the Trinity he did nevertheless present an elaborate and somewhat confusing example of two mirrors set up to face one another, reflecting the same image back and forth, as an analogy for the relationship between the distinct *aqānīm* of the one God.[91] One suspects that the complexity, and the physics involved, is what appealed to the philosopher in this instance.

Somewhat unexpectedly, Yaḥyā also furnished some interesting details in his essays that allow the modern reader to gain some small insight into the social circumstances of the writer's milieu. For example, in one of his essays on the Trinity, he refers to "Christian *mutakallimūn*,"[92] an expression that one finds almost nowhere else, but that signifies Christian participation in an important intellectual undertaking of the time. In another

89. Périer, *Petits traits apologétiques*, 53.

90. Ibid., 25.

91. See ibid., 11–23.

92. Ibid., 39.

essay Yaḥyā gives a reason for the problem he and presumably other Christian scholars had in explaining the doctrine of the Trinity to the Muslims. He says the problem is ignorant Christians who themselves think that "the three *aqānīm* are three essences, subjects, each one of which differs from its two companions in itself, . . . a sin and an infidelity [*kufrun*], by means of which they are requiring the Creator, exalted be His name, to be three substances and three gods!"[93] One supposes that with this allegation Yaḥyā had some misled local "Nestorians" in mind. Nevertheless, in the same essay he refers several times to "the three sects of Christians," and to what he calls the consensus (*ijmā'*) of the Christians in Trinitarian doctrine.[94]

III

Thus far we have presented the Qur'ān, and the Islamic tradition after it, as rejecting the classical Christian doctrine of the Trinity, the Christian "three," as virtual, but unwitting unbelief (*kufr*), and we have reviewed the three trajectories along which Arabic-speaking Christians living in the Islamic world from about 750 to 1050 pursued their defense of the reasonableness of the doctrine. It is time now to ask what significance this excursus in Eastern Christian historical theology might have for Western Christian theology in the twenty-first century.

In the first place, it is necessary to emphasize the point that the Qur'ān's critique of the "Christian three" is in fact concerned with the doctrine of the Trinity as it was confessed by the local "Melkites," "Jacobites," and "Nestorians" in the simple expression that the one God is Father, Son, and Holy Spirit. The Christians who lived among the Muslims in the early Islamic period clearly recognized this fact, and so did a number of contemporary Muslim writers. One must insist on this point because it has become popular among some Western scholars in recent years to suppose that the Christian doctrines criticized by the Qur'ān and the early Muslims were not those of the local mainline churches, but reflections of the views of earlier, more peripheral Christian communities. For example, some say that according to the Qur'ān the Christian Trinity consists of some such triad as God, the Virgin Mary, and Jesus.[95] The fact is that the Qur'ān, with

93. Ibid., 45.

94. See ibid., 55–62.

95. See, for example, most recently, Hans Küng, *Der Islam: Geschichte, Gegenwart, Zukunft* (München: Piper, 2004) 605.

its rhetoric of critique, upbraids the Christians for exaggerating their religion by saying that the one God is Jesus the Messiah, while the Qur'ān itself corrects this exaggeration with its own statement that he, Jesus, Mary's son, is rather God's Word and a Spirit from Him (IV *an-Nisā* 171). And this criticism is still the one to which Christians must respond in any theology adequately developed to meet the actual Islamic challenge, following the example of the Arabic-speaking theologians whose defense of the "Christian three" we have reviewed.

In contrast to most Western theologians, both medieval and modern, Arabic-speaking Christians living in the world of Islam have all along had an adequate and accurate idea of the teachings of the Qur'ān, and they have had an adequate and accurate understanding of early Islamic theology. As we have seen, they engaged with Muslim thinkers on their own terms in the effort to commend the credibility of the Christian doctrines that the Muslims questioned. The now anonymous Christian author of the so-called *On the Triune Nature of God* used the Qur'ān itself, in addition to the Jewish and Christian scriptures, to commend the credibility of belief in the one God, Father, Son, and Holy Spirit. The Christian *mutakallim* 'Ammār al-Başrī argued in his Arabic *kalām* treatises in support of the veracity of the Christian doctrine of "trining" or "trebling" (*at-tathlīth*) the "oneness" (*waḥdāniyyah*) of God by arguing that the doctrine shows the way out of the conundrum that faced the Muslim *mutakallimūn* of his time in the controversy over the ontological status of the one God's essential attributes, attested in the scriptures. The Christian logician and peripatetic philosopher of Baghdad Yaḥyā ibn 'Adī, like the Muslim philosophers before him, al-Kindī and al-Fārābī in particular, investigated the meaning of the predicate "one" (*al-wāḥid*) as it is reasonably affirmed of the Creator, in order satisfactorily to demonstrate that the Creator may logically and most credibly be described from one perspective as "one" being/substance (*jawhar/ousia*), and from another perspective as three *aqānīm* or "hypostases."

A Christian critic, writing from the perspective of the earlier Greek (or Latin) theologies, may wonder about the ontological adequacy of the concepts of the Arabic "attributes" (*sifāt*), or "meanings/referents" (*ma'ānī*), or "properties" (*khawāṣṣ*) of the divine being to express the full reality of the divine "hypostases" or "persons" as confessed by orthodox Nicene Christians. But it is nevertheless clear that this is the very confession the Arabic-speaking apologists were translating not only into Arabic, but into the theological idiom of Islamic religious discourse. This discourse provided the intellectual template for the development of a new Christian apologetics. It is true that given the vicissitudes of Christian life in the world of Islam after the thirteenth century, the development of Christian thought in Arabic suffered an arrest. But by then the lines of its distinctive contours had been drawn, and one can find them still in texts published by Arabic-speaking Christians in our own time.

But what has all this to do with Christian theology in the twenty-first-century West? Is it just a matter of a somewhat recondite historical curiosity? Given the fact that such a Christian engagement with Islamic thought for the sake of Christian theology itself never happened in the West, it seems to me that the history of Arab Christian thought has a strong potential to show the way to modern Western theology now challenged by Islam from within, and not just from outside the Western world. In spite of its medieval engagement with Arabic philosophy, and the familiarity of the names of Avicenna, Averroes, or even al-Ghazzalī to Christian thinkers, the West has seldom seen a serious theological engagement with mainstream Islamic religious thought. A spectacular early example may be the enterprise of the ill-fated Ramón Llull (1235–1315), or even the vigorous approach of Nicholas of Cusa (1401–1464).[96] But the effort to commend Christian faith in Islamic terms has yet to be tried in the West, albeit that there have been Western Christians deeply immersed in the religious lore of the world of Islam, people like Louis Massignon (1883–1962) who have found ways to deepen their Christian faith in their experience of Islam.[97]

The fact is that Islam presses Christianity precisely on the major points of its articles of faith. Christian theology, always apologetic in major ways, faces an old challenge in a new idiom. It is worth remembering that the fourth- and fifth-century articulations of Christian faith were themselves elaborated precisely to express the articles of faith in the idiom of late antique Hellenism. In the modern Western world, Islam, along with other currents of thought, is similarly demanding an explanation from confessing Christians. And in this situation, the Christians themselves might be the chief beneficiaries of the effort. In this era of interreligion, Christian theology must conform itself to the mainlines of the besetting challenges successfully to counter them.

96. See Gaudeul, *Encounters and Clashes*, 1:179–82 and 211–13.

97. See, in particular, Louis Massignon, *Les trois prières d'Abraham* (Paris: Cerf, 1997).

So far in Western theology the one major thinker who addressed the challenge of absolute monotheism in terms that Muslim *mutakallimūn* might comprehend has been Karl Rahner, in his essay, "Einzigkeit und Dreifaltigkeit Gottes im Gespräch mit dem Islam."[98] While Rahner seems not to have been conversant with either the Islamic or the Christian *kalām*, one supposes that he would have found the thought of ʿAmmār al-Baṣrī congenial, especially the latter's rejection of the potentially misleading term "person," and his insistence on proper definitions of technical terms like "hypostasis" or *uqnūm*.

Following the cue of the Arabic-speaking theologians who did Christian theology in the early Islamic period, it seems that the modern Western theologian, newly brought into the thought-world of the Qur'ān and the religious thinking of Muslims, would do well first to approach it from the perspective of comparative theology and from that vantage point to discern what patterns of thought offer the best opportunity both for commending the credibility of Christian faith and for enriching Christian theology.[99] In a world in which an inclusive and materialist secularism undermines theism on all sides, it may be that within their substantial and enduring differences, the monotheist traditions still have much to learn from one another.

98. Karl Rahner, *Schriften zur Theologie*, ed. Paul Imhof (Zürich: Benziger, 1978) 13:129–47; English translation in Karl Rahner, *Theological Investigations*, trans. Edward Quinn (New York: Crossroad, 1983) 18:105–21.

99. See, e.g., Klaus von Stosch, "Der muslimische Offengarungsanspruch als Herausforderung komparativer Theologie: Christlich-theologische Untersuchungen zur innerislamischen Debatte um Ungeschaffenheit und Präexistenz des Korans," *Zeitschrift für katholische Theologie* 128 (2006) 53–74.

2

Abū Rā'iṭa al-Takrītī and God's Divine Pedagogy

Sandra Keating

I. Introduction

WHEN I BEGAN RESEARCH in the fairly obscure field of ninth-century Christian Arabic theology over fifteen years ago, I was not primarily concerned with the "relevance" of the topic. In fact, many of my fellow graduate students had convinced me that falling into the trap of trying to make my research relevant would compromise the integrity of the work. Consequently, it was a great surprise to me to discover the usefulness of insights gained by theologians over a thousand years ago for contemporary reflections on the relationship between Muslims and Christians.

I have in the past decade often been asked privately and publicly to what extent I think Islam is a threat to Western or Christian civilization—will Islam overcome Christianity? On reflection, I have come to believe that this question misses the point and that St. Augustine's insights explicated in his *City of God* concerning the fall of the Roman Empire should be taken to heart, first and foremost, that the rise and fall of societies in human history should not be equated with setbacks and successes in salvation history. The question is not what threat Islam presents to human institutions or values Christians hold near and dear, but rather how God is calling us in this particular moment in time to rise to the challenges presented by what some have called "alternative truth claims."

What has perhaps been most surprising to me is the similarity of the situation in early ninth-century Iraq to our own, not in any superficial or obvious way, but in the constraints and responsibilities that many Christians felt every day. They had lived in a world that was socially, linguistically, and religiously diverse. They had reached a certain *modus vivendi* with a multitude of Christian sects. Suddenly, with the Arab conquest and the unexpected stabilization of a growing Muslim culture, they were faced with changes in their everyday landscape that challenged their religion, language, and way of life. Simultaneously their response was hindered by legal and social limits. One can see many different reactions to the situation—military resistance, emigration, assimilation, etc. A small group of these people, perhaps one might characterize them as "intellectuals," responded to the new context with a deep engagement of the ideas presented by the confluence of these various streams of culture and produced a brilliant flowering of civilization.[1]

I do not in any way mean to imply that the transition and engagement took place in a peaceful vacuum—destruction of life, property, and culture during this period is well documented. Rather, I wish to draw attention to the manner in which some Christians approached the challenge of Islam and the opportunity it presented. I think these challenges and opportunities are again at hand, and for this reason the "relevance" of the ninth century becomes apparent for us.

In my paper I wish to offer some of my own reflections on how one Christian apologist, Abū Rā'iṭa al-Takrītī, responded to the growing presence of Islam in Iraq at the turn of the ninth century. Although many of you may be skeptical that the insights of someone who lived over a millennium ago could apply to our extremely complex situation today, I will suggest

1. For an excellent overview of the early rise of the Islamic state and the Christians living within the Muslim context, see Marshall G. S. Hodgson, *The Venture of Islam: Conscience and History in a World Civilization*, 3 vols. (Chicago: University of Chicago Press, 1974), esp. vol. 1, and Richard Bell, *The Origin of Islam in Its Christian Environment: The Gunning Lectures, Edinburgh University, 1925* (London: Macmillan, 1926). Intellectual ferment and the translation movement is well described in Dimitri Gutas, *Greek Thought, Arabic Culture: The Graeco-Arabic Translation Movement in Baghdad and Early 'Abbāsid Society (2nd–4th/8th–10th Centuries)* (London: Routledge, 1998).

that his method of apology can form the foundation for a fruitful way to speak with clarity about our own beliefs in the engagement with Islam.

II. Abū Rā'iṭa al-Takrītī

Habīb ibn Hidma Abū Rā'iṭa was, as he describes himself, a member of the so-called Jacobite church (i.e., the Syrian Orthodox church) who died around the year 830 in or near the city of Takrīt in Iraq. Although very little is known about him personally, his theological writings are among the very first in Arabic that can be connected to a named person.[2] Abū Rā'iṭa was unknown in the Western church until recently, but his writings have been highly regarded by many Christians in the East and were preserved by the Coptic Church.

Later traditions identified him as a bishop of Takrīt or Nisibis, but this is almost certainly not the case. Rather, it is likely that he was a lay theologian, similar to the *malpōnō* in the Nestorian church.[3] In this capacity, his primary obligations would have been to teach and to advise the clergy on theological issues facing the church, and consequently he would have been required to respond to the current crisis brought about by the Muslim occupation of Iraq. Among the many difficulties facing Christians with the ascendency of the 'Abbāsid caliphate were increasing pressures, primarily through social, economic, and legal means, to convert to Islam and to adopt Arabic as their *lingua franca*.[4] Abū Rā'iṭa rose to the challenge and became a well-known apologist for Christianity in Arabic, apparently participating in staged debates that took place among the various religious groups living in and near Baghdad. His extant writings show evidence of his involvement

2. For an overview of Abū Rā'iṭa's life and context, see Sandra Toenies Keating, *Defending the "People of Truth" in the Early Islamic Period: The Christian Apologies of Abū Rā'iṭah*, HCMR 4 (Leiden: Brill, 2006) 1–55.

3. Sandra Toenies Keating, "The Use and Translation of Scripture in the Apologetic Writings of Abū Rā'iṭa al-Takrītī," in *The Bible in Arab Christianity*, ed. David Thomas, HCMR 6 (Leiden: Brill 2007) 259–61.

4. See Richard W. Bulliet, *Conversion to Islam in the Medieval Period: An Essay in Quantitative History* (Cambridge: Harvard University Press, 1979) esp. 81–82; Wadi Z. Haddad, "Continuity and Change in Religious Adherence: Ninth-Century Baghdad," in *Conversion and Continuity: Indigenous Christian Communities in Islamic Lands, Eighth to Eighteenth Centuries*, ed. M. Gervers and R. J. Bikhazin, Papers in Mediaeval Studies 9 (Toronto: Pontifical Institute of Mediaeval Studies, 1990) 34; André Ferré, "Chrétiens de Syrie et de Mésopotamie au début de l'Islam," *Islamochristiana* 14 (1988) 77–79.

in these debates, increasing their value as windows into his complicated times.

Abū Rā'iṭa's writings can be divided into two distinct but, I would argue, closely related categories. The first, probably written closer to the beginning of his career, are concerned with defending Jacobite teachings against the Melkites.[5] He identifies his primary opponent here as the well-known bishop of Ḥarrān, Theodore Abū Qurrah.[6] The second group is focused on questions raised by Muslims about Christian doctrine and practice and gives advice on how best to answer them.[7] Although his writings might seem to address separate challenges (in theology today this is a given), Abū Rā'iṭa sees the two audiences of his apologetical exercises as inextricably bound together, since the issues debated among Christian sects are thrown into a particular relief when one is confronted with a fundamental challenge to Christian belief.

In each of his texts he writes with all of his potential readers—Muslim, Melkite, and Jacobite—in mind. As a consequence, Abū Rā'iṭa approaches Islam as both a challenge and an opportunity to present Christian teaching to non-Christians, as well as to build coherent responses to new aspects of questions that were explored by previous generations of Christian

5. Four of these texts are extant: "In refutation of the Melkites concerning the Union [of the divinity and humanity in Christ]"; "The third *Risāla* of Abū Rā'iṭa al-Takrītī giving evidence for the threefold praise of the one who was crucified for us"; "On evidence for the threefold praise of the one who was crucified for us"; and "Refutation of the Melkites." Several very brief excerpts from his writings, both extant and lost, are found in the eleventh-century Copto-Arabic compilation *Kitāb iʿtirāf al-ābā'*, "The book of the confession of the Fathers." See the collection of Abū Rā'iṭa's writings in *Die Schriften des Jacobiten Ḥabīb Ibn Hidma Abū Rā'iṭah*, ed. and trans. Georg Graf, CSCO 130 (Arabic text) and 131 (German trans.) (Louvain: L. Durbecq, 1951).

6. Sidney H. Griffith is the author of numerous studies of Theodore Abū Qurrah, including "Muslims and Church Councils: The Apology of Theodore Abū Qurrah," *Studia Patristica* 25 (Leuven: Peeters, 1993) 270–99; "Reflections on the Biography of Theodore Abū Qurrah," *Parole de l'Orient* 18 (1993) 143–70; and "Theodore Abū Qurrah, the Intellectual Profile of an Arab Christian Writer of the First Abbasid Century," The Dr. Irene Halmos Chair of Arabic Literature Annual Lecture (Tel Aviv: Tel Aviv University, 1992).

7. These include the extant "On the proof of the Christian religion and the proof of the Holy Trinity"; "On the Holy Trinity"; "On the Incarnation"; "Witnesses from the words of the Torah and the prophets and the saints"; "Demonstration of the authenticity of Christianity"; and "Christological Discussion." References have been found to at least two relevant texts now lost: "The second *risāla* from the three *rasā'il* in which he talks about the Holy Trinity and the Incarnation" and "His *risāla* to those of Baḥrīn, of the Christians of the West." See Abū Rā'iṭah, *Schriften* (edition and German translation) and Keating, *Defending* (edition and English translation).

theologians. His aim is to clarify doctrine in a way that can also be useful for Christians debating the best expression of the truths of their faith. Abu Ra'ita is an apologist in the traditional sense, but he does not simply offer a "defense" of Christianity. Rather, he develops a way to demonstrate the coherence of Christian doctrine in light of the new challenge of Islam—he strengthens the faith of his co-religionists and presents the Christian witness to the truth of Jesus Christ in a manner understandable to his non-Christian readers.

III. Abū Rā'iṭa's Contribution to the Theological Debate with Muslims

Several modern scholars have examined the numerous contributions made by Abū Rā'iṭa toward developing a theological approach to Islam. One that has been noted by many is the manner in which he draws a connection between Patristic reflections on the persons of the Trinity and the debate current at his time among Muslim scholars concerning the divine attributes (*ṣifāt allah*).[8]

This important contribution, however, is a part of Abū Rā'iṭa's larger project of responding to the Muslim claim that the Jewish and Christian scriptures have been tampered with and therefore are unreliable, a charge commonly called *taḥrīf*.[9] One can identify a subtle yet conscious effort

8. See, for example, Harald Suermann, "Trinität in der islamisch-christlichen Kontroverse nach Abū Rā'iṭah," *Zeitschrift für Missionswissenschaft und Religionswissenschaft* 74 (1990) 219–29, and "Der Begriff Ṣifah bei Abū Rā'iṭah," in *Christian Arabic Apologetics during the Abbasid Period (750–1258)*, ed. S. K. Samir and Jørgen S. Nielsen (Leiden: Brill, 1994) 157–71; Salim Daccache, "Polémique, logique et elaboration théologique chez Abū Rā'ita al-Takrītī," *Annals de Philosophie* 6 (1985) 33–88; Sidney H. Griffith, "Comparative Religion in the Apologetics of the First Christian Arabic Theologians," *Proceedings of the PMR Conference* 4 (1979) 63–87, and "Ḥabīb ibn Ḥidmah Abū Rā'iṭah, a Christian *mutakallim* of the First Abbasid Century," *Oriens Christianus* 64 (1980) 161–201; and M. N. Swanson, "The Trinity in Christian-Muslim Conversation," *Dialogue: A Journal of Theology* 44 (2005) 259–60.

9. In several verses the Qur'ān asserts that the People of the Book have altered (*yuḥarrifūna*) the words (e.g., Sura 5:13) and substituted (*tabdīl*) other words (Sura 2:59; 7:162). Other verses explain this more explicitly, identifying several types of alteration including forgetting the revelation (*nisyān*) and generally misinterpreting (*labs*) it or manipulating (*layy*) it to hide (*kitmān*) its true meaning (e.g., 2:42, 140, 174; 3:71, 78; 4:46; 5:13–14; 753, 162, and others). For Abū Rā'iṭa's approach to the problem, see my article "Refuting the Charge of *Taḥrīf*: Abū Rā'iṭah (d.ca. 835) and His 'First Risāla on the Holy Trinity,'" in *Ideas, Images, and Methods of Portrayal: Insights into Classical Arabic*

throughout all of Abū Rā'iṭa's writings to give the "proof" (*burhān*) the Qur'ān (Sura 2:111; 28:75) claims will be demanded on the Day of Judgment for Christian beliefs that it regards as the consequence of human innovation. As a result, he commonly turns first to logic and reason to establish the consistency of Christian doctrine, subsequently adding scriptural passages and references to the Fathers to support his argumentation. I have outlined Abū Rā'iṭa's approach to the charge of *taḥrīf* more thoroughly elsewhere; for our purposes it is important to note that he recognizes that a traditional apologetical response to Muslim concerns can only be successful if one can first establish the logical coherence and continuity of the Old and New Testaments. This is not a new problem. St. Paul expends some energy on just this topic.

But a particular problem confronting Christians in Abū Rā'iṭa's day (indeed one facing any Christian in conversation with Muslims!) was how to account for the continuity between what had been taught by Abraham, Moses, and in the Hebrew scriptures in general, and what had come to be recognized among Christians as authentic expressions of doctrine. The Qur'ān explicitly mentions belief in the Trinity, the incarnation, and the abandonment of certain aspects of Jewish law (circumcision, prohibition against eating pork, etc.)[10] as the result of later human manipulations, intentional or accidental. Further, Abū Rā'iṭa seems to be especially aware that the christological controversies taking place between the third and the seventh centuries and the resultant divisions within the Christian community had lent credence to Muslim claims that Christians had been led off the "straight path" and that the coming of the Qur'ān was a necessary reminder to the "People of the Book."[11] He is not in favor of passing over the theological conflicts among Christians for the sake of appearances, though. Rather, a strong undercurrent that can be identified in all of his writings, no matter the intended readership, is to provide a clear, rational defense of Christian doctrine, its coherence and its continuity throughout the centuries.

Literature and Islam, ed. Sebastian Guenther (Leiden: Brill, 2005) 35–60. An overview of the issue of falsification of the scripture can be found in Ignazio Di Matteo, "Il 'taḥrīf' od alterazione della Bibbia secondo i musulmani," *Bessarione* 26 (1922) 64–111, 223–60; and the first part of Martin Accad, "The Gospel in the Muslim Discourse of the Ninth to the Fourteenth Centuries: An Exegetical Inventorial Table," (four parts) *Islam and Christian-Muslim Relations* 14 (2003) 67–81, 205–20, 337–52, 459–69.

10. E.g., Sura 3: 64–80; 4:171; 5:17,73 and others.

11. Those whom the Qur'ān acknowledges as having received authentic revelations before Muḥammad, including the Jews, Christians, and an unknown group identified as the Sabī'a (e.g., Sura 2:62).

IV. Divine Pedagogy

Abū Rā'iṭa does not always make his argument explicitly, but rather leads his reader to a logical conclusion based on premises that he believes are evident to all who enter into the conversation with an open heart. In his letter sent via the Archdeacon Nonnus of Nisibis to the Armenian Prince Ashōt Msaker sometime around 815,[12] he points to the traditional argument concerning the Christian understanding of how salvation history unfolds before us. In this rather brief letter, he outlines first the continuity between the Old Covenant and the New, emphasizing that

> none of the Believers are guilty [of sin] if they follow the preaching and teaching of the Apostles, that the one God who is revealed (named) in the Old Covenant is the Father, the Son and the Holy Spirit who are revealed in the New Covenant. For the New Covenant conforms and agrees with the Old Covenant in its teaching, it does not negate it, but rather attests to it and confirms it in its profession of the Oneness of God, praise to Him! while explaining and making manifest the Holy Trinity and replacing the Commands of the Old Covenant with what is incomprehensibly and immeasurably better (§3).[13]

This is not in any way a new idea—it is found in St. Paul's letters to the Galatians and the Romans, in the Letter to the Hebrews, and in the writings of Justin Martyr and Irenaeus of Lyon, just to name a few. Yet in this context Abū Rā'iṭa draws specific attention to certain aspects of the Christian view of salvation history that can provide the *burhān* demanded in the Qur'ān. For example, his use of the term "abrogation" (*nāsikh*) would call to mind the Islamic exegetical principle based in the Qur'ān (Sura 2:106; 22:52; 17:86; 13:39; 57:6–7; 16:101), by which certain verses given to Muḥammad are modified or revoked (*mansūkh*) by other verses. This is often the case when a later revelation gives a contradictory or more specific directive.[14]

12. Apparently Abū Rā'ṭah had been invited to Armenia to debate Theodore Abū Qurrah concerning the differences between the Melkite and Jacobite churches. For an unknown reason, Abū Rā'iṭa was not able to make the journey and sent his relative Nonnus on his behalf. From contemporary historical references, one might surmise that Ashōt Msaker was looking westward to the Byzantines for help in his battle against Islamic conquest, and at least briefly considered conversion in the hope of attaining aid. According to Armenian and Syriac sources, Nonnus won the day and the Armenians maintained their monophysite doctrines. See Keating, *Defending*, 35–40.

13. *Schriften*, 130, p. 67.

14. Among the most well known of these is the verse allowing an exception for

Abū Rā'iṭa, however, presents the Christian understanding of abrogation as a process of continuity, not of repudiation. Through his explanation of God's gradual revelation of the divine will to humanity, he is making a subtle and traditional argument that salvation history is a continuous unfolding of God's plan that culminates in Jesus Christ. Elements of the revelation that were intended to teach and form God's people may now have become obsolete (such as certain dietary laws), but this does not imply a discontinuity: God's revelation "builds" on what came before it until the resurrection of Christ, when the divine plan was fully disclosed.

Abū Rā'iṭa applies this idea to the relationship between the Old and New Covenants (and their respective revelations) and the first three ecumenical councils. Here, he presents salvation history as the unfolding of God's plan, or "call" (*da'wā*), which is continuous and interwoven. The progress of history toward its culmination persists in drawing human beings into a deeper knowledge of previous teachings, and preparing for what is to come (§3). He argues that the fullness and perfection of revelation is known to humanity gradually over generations. At each stage it is guided by the triune God, and so can be trusted, even when the divine threeness had not yet been revealed (§3). In this, Abū Rā'iṭa's approach is similar to the idea of divine pedagogy found in the Fathers that likened the relationship between God and humanity to that of a parent rearing a child.[15] In his own letter, Abū Rā'iṭa extends the principle to show that the conclusions of the first three ecumenical councils truly express truths already present in the very first revelations of God to humanity.

Abū Rā'iṭa's purpose here is twofold: besides providing a brief outline of faith recognizable to his Christian hearers, Muslims would have identified this synopsis as a refutation of the Qur'ānic understanding of God's revelation. The Qur'ān presents God's Word as a single, complete revelation

Muḥammad to marry his adopted son Zayd's former wife, Zaynab (Sura 33:37–38).

15. This idea appears first in the writings of Justin Martyr and Irenaeus concerning the role of Greek philosophy as a preparation for the Gospel and is clearly developed in Clement of Alexandria's *Stromateis* 1 and 7, as well as his *Paedagogus* (PG 8, cols. 247ff.). Later, Cyril of Alexandria (*De adoratione in spiritu et veritate* 13, *Commentarius in Is.* 1 and 3, and *Explanatio in Pss.* 24.4) and Gregory of Nyssa (*Homiliae in orationem dominicam* 5 and *De vita Mosis*) take up the theme of God's instruction and preparation for Christ through Mosaic law. For an overview of divine pedagogy in the writings of Justin Martyr, Irenaeus, and Cyril of Alexandria, see Chrys Saldanha, *Divine Pedagogy: A Patristic View of Non-Christian Religions* (Rome: LAS, 1984). Both Cyril and Gregory were highly regarded by the Jacobite community, and they are the writers most referred to directly in Abū Rā'iṭa's own works.

that has been sent down previously in numerous discrete instances to various chosen prophets.[16] What is contained in the single revelation eternally present on the Preserved Tablet (the *Lawḥ maḥfūẓ* in *Sura* 85:22 and the *Umm al-Kitāb* in 43:4) has now been sent down in the Qur'ān and is the sum total of God's communication to humanity—no more and no less is needed. Muḥammad and his followers, however, quickly became aware that serious discrepancies existed between his message and the scriptures of the Jews and Christians. Muslims answered this problem with the claim that other prophets had received the same revelation, but it had been distorted and corrupted by their followers, the state of affairs identified in the Qur'ān as *taḥrīf* and discussed above. Thus, where the Qurān contradicts the Torah and the Gospels, it acts as a corrective, and as the final revelation according to Muslim teaching, it replaces everything that has come before it.

Christian writers in the early 'Abbāsid period knew that the principal argument made by Muslims against Christian teachings was that they contradicted the message of the prophets as it was presented in the Qur'ān, especially that of Moses and Jesus. Using the Qur'ān as the authoritative source for Jesus' message, they maintained that Christian doctrine concerning the divinity of Christ and the Trinity were the result of distortions introduced by early followers of Jesus (e.g., Sura 5:116–18), especially Paul, and the manipulations of Byzantine emperors acting through church councils. Muslims further argued that the numerous sects of Christianity could be traced to the disagreements resulting from false teachings about Jesus (e.g., Sura 3:70–71; 43:65), which they identified as originating from the councils.[17] According to the Qur'ān, it is exactly the discontinuity among the Torah, the Gospels, and itself that is the proof that the revelation has been tampered with. Furthermore, Muslims could point to specific verses in the Qur'ān that identified Christian belief in the Trinity, the divinity of

16. See, for example, references to the revelation first to Moses (Sura 23:49; 25:35; 37:117), then to Jesus (19:30), and finally to Muḥammad as an "*Arabic Qur'ān*" which is a "clear Book" (43:2–3).

17. Griffith, "Muslims," 282–83. Two centuries later, 'Abd al-Jabbār gave a full account of the traditional Muslim teaching which accurately coincides with information found in other writers of Abū Rā'iṭa's day. See the studies done by S. M. Stern, "Quotations from Apocryphal Gospels in 'Abd al-Jabbār," *Journal of Theological Studies* 18 (1967) 34–57, and "'Abd al-Jabbār's Account of How Christ's Religion was Falsified by the Adoption of Roman Customs," *Journal of Theological Studies* 19 (1968) 128–85.

Christ, and various practices (such as monasticism) as having been "added" to the original revelation and as contrary to the will of God.[18]

Finally, and equally significantly for the argument against Christianity, was the Islamic idea that God's revelation is a "clear Book" (Sura 43:2), which is accessible to everyone without the need for outside sources to understand it. This was believed to be the case for all revelations given to the prophets, including the message brought by Jesus (referred to in the "clear signs" in 43:63), as well as that received by Muḥammad. According to many Islamic scholars of Abū Rā'iṭa's day, the self-evidence of God's revelation meant that only a minimal amount of interpretation, with little reliance on human reason, is necessary for a proper understanding of the revelation received by the prophets. Those who were most skeptical of the abilities of reason saw a danger in the application of "foreign" philosophy to theology, and recognized the seduction of reason as a trap into which Christians had fallen.[19] Consequently, one could argue that gatherings like the Christian councils and synods were neither necessary nor desirable, since they placed undue trust in the ability of unguided human reason to arrive at knowledge of the truth.

These claims demanded that Christians put forward a clear explanation first of the integrity of the Scriptures and second of the coherence of conciliar pronouncements in light of scriptural evidence. The special emphasis that Abū Rā'iṭa places at the beginning of his letter to Ashōt Msaker on the reliability of the Scriptures and the preaching of the apostles concerning the Trinity reveals his attention to Muslim criticism. In the brief opening statements of his letter, he offers an explanation of Christian faith that seeks to make sense out of God's gradual revelation of salvation history, apparent deviations from Judaism and contradictions in church doctrine with his use of "divine pedagogy." His is an argument against any view accepting a revelation that would deny or overturn what is given in the Old and New Testaments. As counterevidence, he substantiates the validity of Christian teachings with Christ's command to preach that the God of the

18. Especially relevant here are the Qur'ān verses that warn against belief in the Trinity (4:171; 5:73), record Jesus' own denial that he is divine (4:171–2; 5:17,72), and disapprove of monasticism (57:27).

19. This was, for example, an overriding concern for Aḥmad ibn Ḥanbal (780–855) and many of his followers. In the *al-Radd ʿalā 'l-Zanādiqa wal-Jahmīya*, a member of the Ḥanbalite school develops an argument that insists on preserving the integrity of the Qur'ān by rejecting the use of reason guided by philosophical ideas, especially those of the Neoplatonist Jahmīya.

Old Covenant is the Father, Son, and Holy Spirit, and asserts that the seeds of this teaching are found in the Old Testament, only to be fully understood in light of the incarnation.

Abū Rā'iṭa is skillfully making the argument that it was not a human rejection or distortion of God's message that necessitated a corrective revelation, which Muslims believe is the purpose of the Qur'ān. Instead, Christian doctrine reflects the acceptance of an authentic divine revelation that is then followed by more profound instruction as to its meaning. Furthermore, this pedagogy has continued in the gatherings of bishops, facilitated by the faithful and led by the Holy Spirit. Thus, Abū Rā'iṭa establishes the link between the First Covenant with Abraham, to the incarnation, to later conciliar pronouncements through the gradual revelation of the Trinity to humankind (§3). This opening section of the letter is not directed toward his Armenian or Melkite listeners—he was fully aware that the issue among the Christian denominations was not whether the councils were legitimate, but which should be recognized. Muslims, on the other hand, who were watching the domestic squabbles with interest, rejected altogether the validity of such conciliar pronouncements as expressions of truth. It was to these observers that Abū Rā'iṭa was speaking here.

Abū Rā'iṭa's writings express several underlying concerns, sometimes expressed explicitly, but often implicitly. At the beginning of several texts, he explains that his intention is to provide his Christian reader with specific arguments and—more importantly, in my opinion—a method for responding to Muslim questions about various Christian doctrines and practices. Read as a complete corpus, a further aspect of his second purpose becomes quite evident—to give confidence to Christians that their faith is not misguided, incoherent, or even false as the Qur'ān claims. He is well aware of the attractiveness of Islam to many Christians because of its simplicity and rejection of complicated creeds and practices; the ease of divorce, remarriage, and polygamy; the negative pressure coming from taxation and legal restrictions placed on non-Muslims; and so on. Thus, it is imperative that Abū Rā'iṭa offer encouragement to those who are being tempted to conversion and questioning the truth of their faith. He does so by showing the consistency and reliability of the Old and New Testaments, and by reminding his readers of the difficulties faced by earlier Christians and Jesus' own encouragement to them.

A third, although perhaps not final, concern that we today should take to heart is the poor witness that disharmony among Christians presents to the Muslim community. Abū Rā'iṭa certainly does not advocate simply ignoring theological disagreements among Christians in an effort to present a unified front in the face of Muslim critiques, yet he is clearly aware that the divisions resulting from arguments among Melkites, Nestorians, and Jacobites have sown doubt in the minds of many. This gives him a further challenge—to present Christian doctrine in such a way as to demonstrate its coherence while simultaneously acknowledging the significance of the christological disputes. In answer to each of these issues Abū Rā'iṭa draws on logical arguments, scriptural passages, and evidence taken from the church fathers. He uses methods employed by his predecessors to construct arguments responding to Jewish and pagan opponents. Nonetheless, what is unique in Abū Rā'iṭa's context is the very specifically Muslim challenge to Christian doctrine: how can we be sure that the God who was revealed to Abraham, Isaac, and Jacob is indeed the same God whom Christians claim is a Trinity and is revealed in the incarnation of Jesus Christ in light of the Muslim counterclaim that Christians have strayed from the "straight path" revealed in the Qur'ān? He responds to this problem by suggesting that God's guidance does not simply lead humanity to recover what was already revealed, but rather draws us into a deeper understanding of the divine plan that can lead to the unexpected, the "incomprehensibly and immeasurably better."

Conclusion

So, what does all of this have to do with us here? I began this paper with the question of whether Christians today should regard Islam as a threat or as a challenge, and suggested that Abu Ra'ita might have a useful approach to recommend to us. I have already noted that in his own day, there were many different responses given, all of which I believe have parallels today as well. But ultimately his manner of facing Islam as a legitimate challenge to Christian beliefs and his conviction that Christianity can answer the questions posed by Muslims by availing themselves of reason, scripture, and tradition, should remind us that although God's definitive revelation comes through Jesus Christ, we as a human community have not yet explored every aspect of the message, nor have we even thought of all of the questions to be asked.

Abu Ra'ita reminds us that Christians believe that the Holy Spirit has guided our expressions of faith and doctrine, beginning with the Scriptures and continuing throughout the life of the church. Perhaps it is even the case that there is a divine purpose in the diversity of religions that is calling us to think of God's activity in creation in a way we have not done so previously. Abu Ra'ita, while keeping in mind his various Christian and Muslim audiences, his complex historical situation, and all of the resources he has at hand to formulate his response, treats Muslim challenges to Christian faith as a springboard to jump deeper into the meaning of revelation, the incarnation, and the Trinity. In my opinion some of the answers he offers are perhaps too limited, but his method is, I believe, an excellent one.

Put succinctly, we should constantly be asking the question of how challenges to our religious beliefs force us to account for what we had not thought of before. This may seem obvious to many. Yet my own experience has been that the general theological emphasis has been on trying to figure out whether and how God saves Muslims (something I believe lies in God's hands, not ours!) rather than on how God is calling Christians to come to a deeper understanding of the Christian message. This is where I would suggest a concept like divine pedagogy could be helpful. If all of creation is moving toward the culmination of salvation history, in what way does Islam (along with other religious groups) play a role in God's preparation of humanity for the final goal? Islam presents some very particular challenges to Christians, at the heart of which is the question of how we account for the ongoing activity of the Holy Spirit and ultimately of the meaning of history.

In our theologically confusing times, I agree with those who suggest that we consider the revival of apologetics not with the intention of simply defending Christianity against its detractors, but rather as a method by which we can explore those certain aspects of the Christ event that Islam is drawing our attention to in the twenty-first century. I am not referring here simply to values such as community, family, prayer, etc. Rather, we should be continuing to investigate the full implications of the incarnation—how is creation different when God does not just send down a message through his prophet Jesus, but rather becomes fully human and dwells among us? At the very least, it points to an utterly different concept of God's relationship to creation and a profoundly unique manner of divine communication.

In the early ninth century in Iraq, Abu Ra'ita recognized that the best apologetics is a full engagement with the opponent. He knew his questioners and the full implications of their proposal—practically, socially, and theologically. He did not reject the questions, nor did he treat them as irrelevant. Rather, he used the opportunity to present the Christian message in a coherent manner—that the Christian community, with all its divisions, bears witness to the profound reality that the triune God is present among us. This project remains as necessary today as it was in the ninth century.

3

Apology or Its Evasion?

Some Ninth-Century Arabic Christian Texts on Discerning the True Religion

Mark N. Swanson

Introduction

It was early in 1984 that, browsing in the Hartford Seminary library, I stumbled upon an article by Sidney H. Griffith titled "The Concept of *al-uqnum* in 'Ammar al-Basri's Apology for the Doctrine of the Trinity."[1] I had never heard of Griffith before, nor had I heard of 'Ammar, the early ninth-century "Nestorian"[2] theologian who was the subject of the article.

1. Sidney H. Griffith, "The Concept of *al-uqnum* in 'Ammar al-Basri's Apology for the Doctrine of the Trinity," in *Actes du premier congrès international d'études arabes chrétiennes (Goslar, septembre 1980)*, ed. [Samir] Khalil Samir, Orientalia Christiana Analecta 218 (Rome: Pontificium Institutum Studiorum Orientalia, 1982) 169–91. A slightly adapted version of this essay, with the same title, was published in *Currents in Theology and Mission* 37:5 (October 2010): 389–99. The present version is published here with the permission of the editors of that journal.

2. That is, a member of the (Antiochian, dyophysite) Church of the East. The label

But I read the article—and was thrilled. Griffith demonstrated beyond any shadow of a doubt that ʿAmmar's Trinity-discourse was no mere translation of earlier Greek or Syriac material, but was part of a conversation with Muslim dialectical theologians, the *mutakallimun*. Some of these theologians had tied themselves into intellectual knots in their attempts to square the Islamic doctrine of God's unicity with the Qur'an's multiple names for God; Griffith mapped out how ʿAmmar, in effect, jumped into the middle of the argument and offered Christian Trinity-discourse as a solution to an Islamic conundrum.[3] Discovering that article was the beginning of my interest in the Arabic Christian theological heritage, and I've been grateful to Father Griffith ever since.

The contributions of Griffith and Keating in the present volume point to the importance of medieval Arabic Christian texts for the ongoing encounter between Christians and Muslims, and the possibility of Christian theology's enrichment through this encounter. In these texts we meet Christian theologians who offered "an accounting for the hope" that was in them, using the very language of the Muslims' sacred Scripture, as well as the vocabulary, tools and arguments of their developing intellectual traditions. We see, in them, Christians who took the challenges of Islam to Christian faith seriously, and responded creatively.

That, it seems to me, is a tradition that the Church needs to explore and celebrate—precisely because so much of the literature of Christian-Muslim relations over the past fourteen centuries does *not* take the challenges of Islam to Christian faith seriously. From John Damascene's description of Islam as the "still-prevailing deceptive superstition of the Ishmaelites, the fore-runner of the Antichrist"[4] to polemical Web sites today, the Christian church does not have a particularly good record of measured theological engagement with Muslims. There are exceptions, as Griffith's and Keating's chapters eloquently attest. But the creative encounters are easy to lose among polemics, eagerly repeated but utterly mendacious legends about the Muslims' Prophet, or neomartyr accounts in which Muslim characters are portrayed as ferocious and immoral.[5] To these one may add apocalyptic

"Nestorian" is understood today to be pejorative, although it was widely used in medieval Arabic texts, both Christian and Islamic.

3. See Griffith's chapter in this volume.

4. Daniel J. Sahas, *John of Damascus on Islam: The "Heresy of the Ishmaelites"* (Leiden: Brill, 1972) 133.

5. Helpful guides to this material include Jean-Marie Gaudeul, *Encounters and Clashes: Islam and Christianity in History*, 2 vols. (Rome: PISAI, 1990); Robert G. Hoyland,

texts, in which events involving Muslims—their building of the Dome of the Rock, for example—are interpreted as signs of the End of Time, and in which Muslims figure into the interpretation of the cast of apocalyptic characters: Gog and Magog, the Abomination of Desolation, the fourth beast of Daniel 7, the locusts of Revelation 9, the seven-headed dragon of Revelation 12, or the Beast whose number is 666 in Revelation 13.[6] The Christian literature occasioned by the encounter with Islam is full of ways of dismissing or demonizing it, and certainly of evading its challenges to Christian doctrine and practice.

In what follows, I would like to describe a very popular apologetic strategy common to three Arabic-speaking theologians, from different regions of Mesopotamia, who flourished in about the first third of the ninth century: Theodore Abu Qurrah, the Melkite (Chalcedonian) bishop of Harran; Habib Abu Ra'itah of Tikrit, the Jacobite (anti-Chalcedonian miaphysite) theologian who is the subject of Professor Keating's essay; and 'Ammar al-Basri (i.e., of Basrah), mentioned above. The strategy they develop is a curious one, and may at first seem to be a sophisticated addition to the list of ways in which Christians have *evaded* Islamic challenges to Christian teachings. In order to get a sense of this, we must turn to some texts.

On the True Religion

One of the most important loci in the controversial literature arising from the Christian-Muslim encounters of the late eighth and ninth centuries is one that we might label "On the true religion." Christian apologists adopted a variety of approaches to this topic. From the time of the very earliest Christian-Muslim debates, as far as we can tell, they identified

Seeing Islam as Others Saw It: A Survey and Evaluation of Christian, Jewish and Zoroastrian Writings on Early Islam, Studies in Late Antiquity and Early Islam 13 (Princeton: Darwin, 1997); and John V. Tolan, *Saracens: Islam in the Medieval European Imagination* (New York: Columbia University Press, 2002).

6. There is a huge literature on this topic. To the works by Hoyland and Tolan in the previous note, it may be interesting to add some studies of Luther: John T. Baldwin, "Luther's Eschatological Appraisal of the Turkish Threat in *Eine Heerpredigt wider den Türken*," *Andrews University Seminary Studies* 33 (1995) 185–202, and Gregory J. Miller, "Luther on the Turks and Islam," *Lutheran Quarterly* 14 (2000) 79–97. Also, for early American missionaries to the Islamic world, see Timothy Marr, *The Cultural Roots of American Islamicism* (Cambridge: Cambridge University Press, 2006) ch. 2, "Drying Up the Euphrates: Muslims, Millenialism, and Early American Missionary Enterprise."

fulfilled prophecy and evidentiary miracles as positive signs by means of which the true religion might be discerned—and tacitly or explicitly called the prophethood of Muhammad into question because of their presumed absence in his career.[7] That the Christian argument was not without effect is clear from the response of Muslim apologists, who sought out prophecies of Muhammad in the Christian scriptures, worked out their own sets of criteria for discerning the true prophet, and developed the doctrine of *i'jaz al-Qur'an*, the sublime inimitability of the Qur'anic speech, which they proposed as Islam's distinctive and unsurpassable evidentiary miracle.[8]

Positive criteria for discerning the true religion *in addition to* fulfilled prophecy and evidentiary miracles are advanced in what may be one of Theodore Abu Qurrah's earliest writings, *On the Existence of the Creator, and the True Religion*.[9] In the heart of this treatise,[10] Theodore claims that the true religion is the one that possesses doctrines in accordance with what human reason can perceive about the nature of God, the moral life, and reward and punishment in the afterlife. Arguing on the basis of analogy with human beings—or at one point even more specifically with prelapsarian Adam, created "in the image of God" (and so making the analogy

7. Already John of Damascus makes the charge that there are no prophecies of the coming of Muhammad; Sahas, *John of Damascus on Islam*, 135. As for Christian insistence on the importance of evidentiary miracles, see below.

8. See Sarah Stroumsa, "The Signs of Prophecy: The Emergence and Early Development of a Theme in Arabic Theological Literature," *Harvard Theological Review* 78 (1985) 101–14. For an excellent example of a ninth-century defense of Islam as the true religion, see A. Mingana, *'Ali Tabari: The Book of Religion and Empire: A Semi-Official Defence and Exposition of Islam Written by Order at the Court and with the Assistance of the Caliph Mutawakkil (A.D. 847–861)* (Manchester: University Press, 1922). On the development of the doctrine of *i'jaz al-Qur'an*, see Richard Martin, "The Role of the Basrah Mu'tazilah in Formulating the Doctrine of the Apologetic Miracle," *Journal of Near Eastern Studies* 39 (1980) 175–89.

9. Edition of the Arabic text: *Théodore Abuqurra: Traité de l'existence du Créateur et de la vraie religion*, ed. Ignace Dick, Patrimoine Arabe Chrétien 3 (Rome: PIO, 1982). English translation: *Theodore Abu Qurrah*, Library of the Christian East 1 (Provo, UT: Brigham Young University Press, 2005) 165–74, 1–25, 41–47. Major study: Sidney H. Griffith, "Faith and Reason in Christian Kalam: Theodore Abu Qurrah on Discerning the True Religion," in *Christian Arabic Apologetics during the Abbasid Period (750–1258)*, ed. Samir Khalil Samir and Jørgen S. Nielsen (Leiden: Brill, 1994) 1–43.

10. Or set of treatises. Note that Lamoreaux treats the work, which circulates as a unity in the known manuscripts, as three separate treatises that he titles *On Natural Theology*, *Theologus Autodidactus*, and *That Christianity Is from God*; Lamoreaux, *Theodore Abu Qurrah*, 165–74, 1–25, and 41–47, respectively. In this essay I am concerned with the second and third parts/treatises.

possible)—Theodore concludes that human mind can perceive the inner-communal nature of God, the imperative of love in this life, and the incorporeal sublimity of reward in the next life. Comparing these conclusions to existing religions (with some unsubtle criticisms of Islamic teaching and practice along the way), Theodore unsurprisingly concludes that of all the candidates in the world for the title of True Religion, Christianity fits best.[11]

A surprising feature of this material is that it is immediately followed by a kind of appendix; John Lamoreaux, in his excellent collection of English translations of Theodore's works, treats it as a separate treatise and gives it the title *That Christianity Is from God*.[12] It begins as follows: "We *also* report that there is *another* way in which our minds can infer that the religion of Christianity is from God . . ."[13] With these words, Theodore introduces an argument for discerning the True Religion that is entirely different from the one just concluded: rather than presenting the positive criteria that indicate the True Religion, he instead presents an analysis of the motives for which a person might decide to choose a religion *other* than the true one.

Theodore's argument goes something like this. After reminding the reader that he is arguing on the basis of *reason*, he summarizes the humanly comprehensible motives for which people might decide to adopt a religion: they might be constrained to do so by the sword; they might embrace the new religion in the hope of gaining wealth, power and status; they might embrace a religion that gives scope to their fleshly passions; or they might find in the new religion theological teachings of which the minds of ordinary people can approve, perhaps because of their simplicity, or because of their familiarity. Theodore goes on to argue that *none* of these reasons can account for the acceptance of Christianity at the hands of the apostles, who coerced no one, who were without status, possessions, strength, or learning, and who called their hearers to lives of asceticism. As for Christianity's theological teachings, the apostles "did not at all call them to faith in a matter about which they had heard, or of which their human minds could approve, or to which anyone had previously called, but rather to a matter that was *new* and *strange*": namely, the incarnation of the Son of God; his virgin birth and human growth; his rejection, suffering, crucifixion, death,

11. Dick, *Traité de l'existence du Créateur et de la vraie religion*, 199–258; Lamoreaux, *Theodore Abū Qurrah*, 1–25.

12. Dick, *Traité de l'existence du Créateur et de la vraie religion*, 259–70; Lamoreaux, *Theodore Abū Qurrah*, 41–47.

13. Dick, *Traité de l'existence du Créateur et de la vraie religion*, 259 (par. 1). All English translations in this essay are the author's, from the published Arabic texts.

and burial; his resurrection after three days and ascension into heaven; and that salvation is solely through faith in him, who is God and Son of God.[14] It is striking that, in describing this "new and strange matter," Theodore comes very close to reciting the second article of the Creed.

But now—moving to the next step of Theodore's argument—if Christianity was not accepted for any of the reasons just mentioned (coercion, worldly gain, license, or easy and familiar doctrines), the secret of Christianity's undisputed spread in the world must lie elsewhere: namely, in the *evidentiary miracles* that accompanied its preaching. For an archetypical example, Theodore recalls a scene from the *Acts* of the Apostle Thomas, who raised a man from the dead "in the name of Jesus Christ, crucified in Jerusalem"—at which point the kings of India, who had previously been mocking the apostle's preaching, came to faith in the crucified and risen Christ.[15]

This might be a place to pause and make a couple of observations about Theodore's argument. On the one hand, it is not particularly convincing. Each item in Theodore's list of humanly comprehensible reasons for accepting a religion—coercion by the sword, worldly gain, license with regard to fleshly appetites, simplified doctrine—corresponds to well-known Christian charges against Islam, and it seems that Theodore's argument is circular from the outset, assuming what it sets out to demonstrate.[16] On the other hand, however, one can admire the sheer audacity of Theodore's argument. He was keenly aware that Muslims found Christian teaching, especially that of the crucifixion of the one confessed to be Lord and God, to be scandalous. In his various writings he reports some vivid epithets that

14. Ibid., 259–64. The translated matter is at 263 (par. 20).

15. Ibid., 264–70. The story of the Apostle Thomas is at 269 (pars. 45–48).

16. In addition, few contemporary students of early Christian history would want to claim that there are no humanly comprehensible motives—be they economic, or sociological, or psychological—for the earliest spread of Christianity. Over the years I have frequently directed church history students to Rodney Stark, *The Rise of Christianity* (Princeton: Princeton University Press, 1996), written with the assumption that the early growth of the Christian movement *is* sociologically comprehensible. People *did* become Christians because of solidarity within networks of family and friends, and out of hope for material well-being and greater social status in this world, as well as felicity in the world to come.

could be flung at the Christians' belief: it is "folly,"[17] "an abomination,"[18] so senseless that "the delirium of sleep is more to the point than their speech."[19] But in this little appendix/treatise, *That Christianity Is from God*, Theodore *incorporates* the sense of scandal and repulsion aroused by this abominable, delirious folly into an argument for its *truth*: this folly is such a stumbling block for the human mind that only divine authentication can account for the observable fact that people throughout the world—the wise, the ignorant, and those in between—actually came to believe it! And, to give this dialectic of paradoxicality one final twist, Theodore points out that it is not just *any* sort of divine demonstration that authenticates the Christian religion, but specifically the miracle of raising the dead *in the name of the Crucified*. Theodore points this out plainly in another little treatise, *On the Confirmation of the Gospel*,[20] where we read:

> [The apostles] did not say to the dead person, "Rise in the name of God!" Rather, they said to him, "Dead one, I tell you in the name of Jesus of Nazareth, whom the Jews crucified in Jerusalem, rise!" And the dead person rose immediately.[21]

The anti-Jewish element that we find here and in many of these texts is a topic for another essay;[22] here I simply want to point out the way in which Theodore builds Christian faith's great paradox, the crucifixion of the one confessed as Lord and God, into both the negative and the positive moments of his argument.

The text from which I have just quoted, *On the Confirmation of the Gospel*, offers a list of humanly comprehensible motives for adopting a

17. *hamaq*, in *Chapters on Prostration to the Icons*: Ignace Dick, ed., *Théodore Abuqurra: Traité du culte des icons*, Patrimoine Arabe Chrétien 10 (Zouk Mikhaël, Lebanon: Patrimoine Arabe Chrétien, 1986) 94 (ch. 2, par. 16). For an English translation of this treatise, see Theodore Abu Qurrah, *A Treatise on the Veneration of the Holy Icons*, trans. Sidney H. Griffith (Louvain: Peeters, 1997).

18. *shana'*, in *On the Law and the Gospel and the Chalcedonian Faith*: Constantine Bacha, ed., *Mayamir Thawudurus Abi Qurrah usquf Harran, aqdam ta'lif 'arabi nasrani* (Beirut: Matba'at al-Fawa'id, 1904) 140–54, here 147. For an English translation of this treatise, see Lamoreaux, *Theodore Abu Qurrah*, 27–39 (ch. 2).

19. *hadhayan al-nawm aqrabu ila l-sadad min kalamihim*, in *Chapters on Prostration to the Icons*: Dick, *Traité du culte des icons*, 92 (ch. 2, par. 11).

20. Edition: Bacha, *Mayamir*, 71–75. English translation: Lamoreaux, *Theodore Abu Qurrah*, ch. 4, 49–53.

21. Bacha, *Mayamir*, 74.

22. See Sidney H. Griffith, "Jews and Muslims in Christian Syriac and Arabic Texts of the Ninth Century," *Jewish History* 3 (1988) 65–94.

religion that is only slightly different from that of *That Christianity Is from God.* In the first place, Theodore lists license or permissiveness; then, might or power; next, ethnic or tribal solidarity; and finally, what he calls "the satisfaction of the mercantile mind."[23] Again, Theodore makes a case that Christianity did *not* spread for any of these reasons: the apostles offered no license to fleshly desires, had no status or might with which to appeal to the worldly ambitious, and attracted a community that developed a new solidarity beyond that of ethnicity, nation, or tribe.[24] Furthermore:

> As for the satisfaction of the fleshly, mercantile mind, it is altogether excluded from the Gospel. That is because the Gospel recalls that Christ, the Son of God, was born of the Father before the ages, and that the Father is not more eternal than he. It recalls that this Son, at the end of time, came down and took up residence in the belly of a woman, and was born from her as a human being, while remaining God as he had been from eternity. He was a child in the manger, he nursed, and grew through eating food until he reached maturity. The Gospel recalls that this eternal Son made offerings to God in the Temple; that Herod sought him, and that he fled from him into Egypt. It recalls that he fasted, was tempted by Satan, and prayed. He hungered, thirsted, and became weary. Fear came upon him, so that he sweated perspiration viscous like blood. His enemies overcame him, insulted him, and put him to shame to the point of spitting in his face. They struck him around his head, scourged him with whips, and crowned him with thorns. They mocked him, nailed his hands and his feet, and hung him from the wood [of the cross]. They gave him vinegar and gall to drink. They stabbed him with a lance, and blood and water burst forth from him. In the course of all that, he called out and said, "My God, my God, why have you forsaken me?"[25]

If in *That Christianity Is from God* Theodore had come close to reciting the Creed at this point in the argument, here in *On the Confirmation of the Gospel* he assembles a whole series of Christ's acts of human weakness, many of which were being used by Muslim controversialists in questions that took the form, "How can you claim for someone who did *this* (fill in the blank), that he is God?"[26] Later Christian apologists would have to

23. *qunuʿ al-ʿaql al-suqi.*

24. Bacha, *Mayamir*, 71–73; Lamoreaux, *Theodore Abū Qurrah*, 49–51.

25. Bacha, *Mayamir*, 73.

26. This is the fundamental question of a text by the ninth-century convert to Islam

write at length about the meaning of Christ's deeds of human weakness, and, in particular, about his prayers, including his prayer in the garden of Gethsemane, or the cry of dereliction from the cross.[27] Theodore, however, boldly and almost preemptively gathers this material into his argument for Christianity's truth.

Up until this point in the argument, Theodore seems to have left open the possibility of saying that while the "fleshly, mercantile mind" may not find Christian teachings persuasive, the minds of the *wise* may find otherwise. But Theodore now slams that door shut: "There is *no one* among the people whose mind can be convinced that God is properly described in such fashion!" And a bit later on, we read, "*No one* is convinced by this or accepts it, not the wise, nor the ignorant, nor the one in between."[28]

We do not know whether Theodore Abu Qurrah was the first to formulate this procedure for discerning the true religion through an analysis of the natural human motives for adopting a religion, and an examination of the available religions in the light of this analysis (a procedure that, for the remainder of this essay, I will simply call "the True Religion apology"). He may well deserve this distinction. Whatever its origins, the procedure quickly became part of the standard apologetic arsenal of Arabic-speaking Christians of every confessional community—as we may see from its use in the writings of Theodore's contemporaries Habib Abu Ra'itah and 'Ammar al-Basri.[29]

Habib Abu Ra'itah begins his treatise *On the Proof of the Christian Religion and the Proof of the Holy Trinity*[30] with the assertion that there are

---

'Ali al-Tabari: his *Refutation of the Christians*. See the French translation of Jean-Marie Gaudeul, *Riposte aux chrétiens par 'Ali Al-Tabari* (Rome: PISAI, 1995), and watch for the new edition and translation of Rifaat Ebied and David Thomas in the Brill series The History of Christian-Muslim Relations [henceforth HCMR].

27. For one example, see Abu Ra'itah's *On the Incarnation*: Arabic text and English translation in Sandra Toenies Keating, *Defending the "People of Truth" in the Early Islamic Period: The Christian Apologies of Abu Ra'itah*, HCMR 4 (Leiden: Brill, 2006) 284–87 (pars. 73–74).

28. Bacha, *Mayamir*, 73–74.

29. The pioneering study of this material is Sidney H. Griffith, "Comparative Religion in the Apologetics of the First Christian Arabic Theologians," *Proceedings of the PMR Conference* 4 (1979) 63–87, reprinted in idem, *The Beginnings of Christian Theology in Arabic*, Variorum Collected Studies Series 746 (Aldershot, UK: Ashgate Variorum, 2002) ch. 1.

30. Arabic text and English translation: Keating, *Defending the "People of Truth,"* 73–145.

seven reasons for the spread of any religion. The first six are: (1) desire with respect to the things of this world; (2) craving for the (corporeal) delights of the world to come; (3) coercing fear; (4) license with respect to desired but forbidden things; (5) what Habib calls approval, *al-istihsan* (to which we shall return in a moment); and (6) collusion and ethnic or tribal solidarity for the purpose of group advancement.[31] Habib comments that these six reasons for the spread of a religion "deviate from the religion of God, have nothing to do with his obedience, and part ways from his religion."[32] But as for the seventh reason for the spread of a religion, it consists in (7) the evidentiary miracles by which God himself establishes the proof of his religion.

Habib's list will now be familiar to us: as in Theodore's lists, we find coercion; desire for worldly gain; permissiveness or license (to which Habib adds the hopes of carnal delights in the world to come); and ethnic or tribal solidarity. And as in Theodore, we find a category that has to do with the religion's doctrines. Theodore, in *That Christianity Is from God*, had spoken of "theological doctrines of which the minds of ordinary people can *approve*"—*tastahsinuha ʿuqul al-ʿammah*;[33] we remember that he had stressed that people would approve *simple* and *familiar* doctrines, but encountered in Christianity matters that were *new* and *strange*. Habib Abu Ra'itah uses the same language of "approval," *al-istihsan*, but in an interestingly different way: he speaks of *al-istihsan li-tanmiqihi wa-zakhrafatihi*, "approval because of [the doctrines'] elegance and ornamentation."[34] In fact, Habib seems to be thinking not so much of one's own approval of doctrines as of the approval that one seeks *for oneself from others* by "putting on" those doctrines, almost as if one were putting on fancy dress clothes in the hope of receiving compliments on one's elegant taste and aesthetic flourishes.

In any event, Habib makes it clear that central Christian teachings are *not* such as to give an air of debonair elegance to those who show them off:

> As for the fifth category, which is the approval [of a belief system] because of its elegance and aesthetic flourishes, this is also inconceivable for the religion of the Gospel. That is because the one who is intended in worship and sought in religious observance; who is the stored-up treasure of the End and hoped-for reward; upon

31. Ibid., 82–95 (pars. 1–10).
32. Ibid., 84 (par. 2).
33. Dick, *Traité de l'existence du Créateur et de la vraie religion*, 260 (par. 7).
34. Keating, *Defending the "People of Truth,"* 88–89 (par. 7).

> whom is reliance in this world and in the next; is a *crucified man*: weak in appearance and despicable to view among his crucifers, who received him with every maltreatment, inexorably culminating in his death and burial.
>
> What sort of "approval" clings to the one who accepts *this*? What ornamentation or elegance attaches to the one who is firmly convinced of *this*?[35]

We move on to our third author, probably the youngest of the three we are considering here, ʿAmmar al-Basri. Two works of his are preserved, *The Book of the Proof* and *The Book of Questions and Answers*; here I will present his argument in *The Book of the Proof.*[36] ʿAmmar's discourse about the True Religion largely follows the pattern we have met in Theodore and Habib, but with some interesting twists. In the first place, while ʿAmmar believes as firmly as Theodore and Habib that the true religion was established by evidentiary miracles, he acknowledges that such miracles had *not* continued down to his own day: once God's true religion was established through God-given signs, they came to an end.[37] Thus there is a historical aspect to ʿAmmar's inquiry: not which of the religions *is* established by evidentiary miracles, but which one *was* so established. He also, later on, will be concerned to alert his readers to the possibility of *counterfeit* signs: for him, one of the "worldly motives" for accepting a religion is what he calls "the illusions and specious proofs of sorcery."[38]

Evidentiary miracles, therefore, are vouchsafed only for a limited period of time, and one must watch out for pale imitations. All the same, they remain central to ʿAmmar's proof for the discernment of the True Religion. He specifically *excludes* the possibility of discerning the True Religion through any capacity of human reason, with all its subtlety and finesse, to scrutinize the teachings and books of the religions in order to distinguish which of them has the truest doctrines. For ʿAmmar, any such attempt goes beyond the limits of what is possible, and lands people "in the sea of God's

35. Ibid., 88–91(par. 7).

36. Edition of Arabic text: Michel Hayek, *ʿAmmar al-Basri: Apologie et controverses*, Nouvelle Série, B. Orient Chrétien 5 (Beirut: Dar el-Machreq, 1977). The *Book of the Proof* occupies pp. 19–90 of the Arabic pagination, with the sections on the True Religion at 24–41.

37. Hayek, *ʿAmmar al-Basri*, 27.

38. Ibid., 39.

knowledge: God has not given them any instrument with which to cross it, and has not commissioned them to plunge into it."[39]

What the human mind can and must do is to examine the religions for the presence of "worldly" or "earthly" motives for their acceptance; one of ʿAmmar's lists includes (1) collusion; (2) the sword; (3) bribes and flattery; (4) ethnic/tribal solidarity; (5) *al-istihsan*, reasoned approval; (6) license with respect to the laws; and (7) the illusions and specious proofs of sorcery, mentioned earlier.[40] By now, such a list should be familiar. Once again, we find the word *al-istihsan* used in connection with the *doctrines* of any particular religion; what ʿAmmar seems to mean by it is the "reasoned approval" of a religion's teachings because of their conformity with notions that human reason can devise and deem acceptable. ʿAmmar writes:

> As for *al-istihsan*, and that which reasoned opinion[41] devises, that arises in thought, and that the mind accepts, with the result that it imagines that this [approval] is a motive for accepting [a religion] apart from evidentiary miracles, I believe that the religion of Christianity is entirely at variance with that. That is because those who called to it called to things and narrated reports that reasoned opinion does *not* devise, that do *not* arise in thought, that do *not* come to mind, and that reason does *not* imagine.[42]

What are these reports? ʿAmmar provides a list of ten: (1) the virginal conception; (2) the virgin birth; (3) that the child that was born was Son of God; (4) that this Son of God was crucified, died, and was buried; (5) that he rose from the grave; (6) that he ascended into heaven; and (7) that he will come again to raise the dead and to judge the righteous and the unrighteous. Following these seven creedal points, ʿAmmar mentions (8) that the apostles called people to the worship of the crucified one, to the bearing of heavy burdens, to distributing their wealth to the poor, to giving their lives over to death for his sake, and (9) to lives of asceticism, without looking for the pleasures of food, drink, and sex either in this life or in the life to come.[43] But ʿAmmar is saving his biggest reason for last:

> The tenth, and it is the summation, perfection and completion of all of this, is that [the Apostles] called [their hearers] to belief

39. Ibid., 27.

40. Ibid., 32–41.

41. "Reasoned opinion" translates *al-raʾy*.

42. Hayek, *ʿAmmar al-Basri*, 36.

43. Ibid., 36–37.

> in a God who is Father, Son, and Holy Spirit. *This* is something that does not arise in thought and that reasoned opinion does not devise. Reasoned opinion may devise Good and Evil on the basis of what people observe of good and evil in the world; or it may devise the One on the basis of what they observe of the order of things, and their witness to One. But as for the Father, the Son and the Holy Spirit, that is *not* something that reasoned opinion devises . . .[44]

When 'Ammar says that "reasoned opinion may devise Good and Evil on the basis of what people observe of good and evil in the world," I believe that he means that reasoned opinion may devise the concept of Good and Evil *principles* or *deities*; in other words, he is saying that it is not surprising that rational people should come up with dualistic religions—and, in a parallel passage in his other book, he mentions the teachings of Zoroaster, Mani, Bardaisan, and Marcion.[45] When 'Ammar says that "reasoned opinion may devise the One on the basis of what they observe of the order of things," I believe he means the One, non-trinitarian, *God*; again, his claim is that it is not surprising that rational people should develop non-trinitarian monotheisms—and in the parallel passage, he explicitly mentions *al-tawhid*, the Islamic term for God's unicity.[46] Human rational analysis may devise and approve of a sheer monotheism, or a dualism, or (as 'Ammar says in the parallel passage) the subtleties of the ancient Greek philosophers, or the doctrines of those who believe in the eternity of the world.[47] 'Ammar suggests that these are religious ideas that plausibly conform in some way to what people observe in the world—and so they may arise in thought, and the mind may give them its approval. But the doctrine of the Trinity is something else again.

Before asking about the significance of this True Religion apology to the wider apologetic enterprise of these writers, I would like to note once again that there are slight differences in emphasis between Theodore's, Habib's, and 'Ammar's speech about *al-istihsan* with regard to a religion's doctrines. Theodore emphasizes a person's ready approval of easy and familiar doctrines—in contrast to which Christianity came with doctrines that were new and strange. Habib's emphasis is on the aesthetic: a person

44. Ibid., 37.

45. In *The Book of Questions and Answers*, Part 2, Question 6: Hayek, *'Ammar al-Basri*, 136.

46. Ibid.

47. Ibid.

may accept doctrines that gain her approval as a person of elegance and refined taste—but Christianity offers a crucified God. 'Ammar emphasizes the mind's reasoned approval of plausible doctrines—and Christianity offers a triune God. In all three cases, the treatment of *al-istihsan* offered the Christian apologist an opportunity to list Christian teachings quite unapologetically, with the paradoxes of the incarnation on vivid display.

The Nature of Their Apologetic Enterprise

What shall we say about all this? The True Religion apology as we find it in Theodore, Habib, and 'Ammar raises some interesting questions and *may* help us better understand the nature of their apologetic enterprise. I shall present my reflections on this matter in a series of five brief points.

1. Exultant, Unapologetic Confession

First, for our ninth-century theologians the True Religion apology provided space for *un*apologetic assertion of the central paradoxes of Christian faith—in particular, the crucifixion and death of the one confessed to be Lord and God. In the passages that we have presented here, Theodore, Habib, and 'Ammar *revel* in the perceived absurdity of Christian faith. At the "Christian Theology and Islam" conference where this essay was first read, more than one participant was reminded of the famous line *credo quia absurdum* (incorrectly) attributed to Tertullian[48]—who *did* write (in Ernest Evans' translation):

> The Son of God was crucified: I am not ashamed—because it is shameful.
> The Son of God died: it is immediately credible—because it is silly.
> He was buried, and rose again: it is certain—because it is impossible.[49]

When writing in "True Religion apology mode," Theodore, Habib, and 'Ammar could speak in similar terms, with similar exultation.

48. Timothy David Barnes, *Tertullian: A Historical and Literary Study* (Oxford: Clarendon, 1971) 223–24.

49. *On the Flesh of Christ*, 5, trans. and ed. Ernest Evans, *Tertullian's Treatise on the Incarnation* (London: SPCK, 1956) 18–19.

2. Giving Away the Store? Hardly!

Precisely thereby, our apologists show themselves to be *uncompromising* Christian theologians, unafraid of stating distinctive Christian teachings in the sharpest possible way. This is an important point to bear in mind, especially when studying other aspects of their apologetic enterprise. Apologetics, after all, are theologically risky, involving (as I once wrote)

> a movement away from faith's own ground, away from its reservoirs of language and narrative and practice. To cite another's scripture is to expose oneself to criticism on the basis of the other's hermeneutics; to use another's language is to risk being understood in quite unintended ways.[50]

We may think again of 'Ammar's attempt to offer Christian Trinity-discourse as a solution to the conundrums of the Muslim *mutakallimun* with regard to the names and attributes of God, and recall that he ended up speaking of God, who exists, and who possesses the essential attributes of Life and Speech.[51] It was a brilliant move, and the resulting apology has been repeated by Arabic-speaking Christians down to the present day. But is it good Christian theology? Since the late nineteenth century in Egypt, a number of theologians, both Coptic Orthodox and Protestant, have protested against this apology. The Trinitarian hypostases *are not attributes*, they have insisted; such discourse has nothing to do either with the Bible or with the Fathers of the Church.[52]

However much these critics may be right on purely theological grounds, I cannot see 'Ammar and others like him as theologians ready to give away the Christian store. Reading his version of the True Religion apology, we see him standing firmly on "faith's own ground," and drinking deeply from "its reservoirs of language and narrative and practice." He may have been willing to venture forth from that ground and those reservoirs, to sojourn in a far country and to drink from others' wells—but not indefinitely. He was a visitor, not an immigrant.

50. Mark N. Swanson, "Ibn Taymiyya and the *Kitab al-burhan*: A Muslim Controversialist Responds to a Ninth-Century Arabic Christian Apology," in *Christian-Muslim Encounters*, ed. Yvonne Yazbeck Haddad and Wadi Zaidan Haddad (Gainesville: University Press of Florida, 1995) 95–107, here 100.

51. See Griffith's chapter in this volume, or his study mentioned in note 1.

52. Mark N. Swanson, "Are Hypostases Attributes? An Investigation into the Modern Egyptian Christian Appropriation of the Medieval Arabic Apologetic Heritage," *Parole de l'Orient* 16 (1990–91) 239–50.

3. Inconsistency?

But now we must ask how the True Religion texts we have read fit into the larger apologetic enterprises of Theodore, Habib, 'Ammar, and others like them. These theologians are known for advancing "reason"—whether the dialectical methods and specific topics of the *kalam*, or the methods and topics informed by the new Arabic translations of Aristotle—as common ground upon which to build an apology.[53] We have already seen, for example, that Theodore asserted over several chapters of his treatise *On the Existence of the Creator and the True Religion* that the True Religion is the one that possesses doctrines *in accordance with what the human mind can perceive* about the nature of God, the moral life, and reward and punishment in the afterlife.[54] While such attempts may occasionally, in the eyes of some, stray too far from scripture or tradition, they at least attempt to render an "accounting for the hope" that sustained their authors (1 Pet 3:15). Over against this, what we have been calling the True Religion apology in effect argues: Christian doctrines are utterly repugnant to reason, and there are no earthly reasons why anyone should believe in them, but people *did* believe in them, and so they must have believed them not for earthly but for heavenly reasons (as confirmed by miracles), and so they must be true! This summary may be a bit of a caricature, but it expresses a nagging suspicion that I have long harbored: that here we find yet *another* way—in addition to the polemics, legends, martyrdoms, and apocalypses mentioned above—in which Christians have managed to evade the challenges of Islam.[55] The True Religion discourse presented here appears to be an apology that undermines apologetics. It is difficult to understand, for example, how Theodore's *That Christianity Is from God* and (the central part of) *On the Existence of the Creator and the True Religion* could circulate in the same manuscript, as parts of a single work. The assumptions of the former (that Christian doctrines are *not* compatible with or acceptable to human reason) seem

53. A brief example of each approach (Theodore Abū Qurrah building on the discourse of the *kalam*, and Habib Abu Ra'itah building on a passage from Aristotle's *Topics*) may be found in Mark N. Swanson, "The Trinity in Christian-Muslim Conversation," *Dialog: A Journal of Theology* 44 (2005) 256–63.

54. Dick, *Traité de l'existence du Créateur et de la vraie religion*, 199–258; Lamoreaux, *Theodore Abū Qurrah*, 1–25.

55. In fact, I titled the first draft of this essay "Evasive Maneuvers." I later dropped this title, partly because I did not want to use a military metaphor (since the study of Christian-Muslim relations is already plagued by them), and partly because I came to see such an evaluation of the True Religion apology as inadequate.

simply to contradict those of the former (that human reason *can* discern correct theological doctrines). Should we conclude, then, that there is a massive inconsistency at the heart of Theodore's apologetic enterprise, and that of his contemporaries?

4. How They Functioned

Here it may be helpful to take a step back, and ask how different forms of Arabic Christian apologetic discourse *functioned* for their first readers and hearers.[56] For example, an apology such as 'Ammar al-Basri's "attribute-defense" of the Trinity (God who exists and possesses the attributes of Life and Speech) may well have served to fend off charges that Christians were tritheists, or that Christian Trinitarian discourse was merely stupid. As for the True Religion apology, it functioned in a rather different way. We remember that Theodore, Habib, and 'Ammar lived at a time and in regions in which rates of conversion to Islam were accelerating, in part because of the pro-conversion policies of the Abbasid rulers who had come to power in 750.[57] Their apologies, and other Arabic Christian texts of the period, were intended at least in part to convince Christians who had adopted the Arabs' *language* not to take the further (and, some might think, logical) step of adopting their *religion*. One can readily imagine that those who crafted True Religion apologies intended to urge Christians who may have been wavering in their Christian allegiance to examine their motives for considering a change in that allegiance, and also to examine the motives of others whom they had seen convert.[58] In addition, theologians such as Theodore, Habib, and 'Ammar regularly wrote their Arabic treatises in the expectation that their work would be read by *Muslim* intellectuals—who might themselves reconsider the motives for which a religion might legitimately be embraced, and perhaps be reminded of the Qur'anic principle that there is "no coercion in religion" (Q 2:116).[59]

56. Such attention to the way texts *functioned* is one of the strengths of Sidney H. Griffith, *The Church in the Shadow of the Mosque: Christians and Muslims in the World of Islam* (Princeton: Princeton University Press, 2008).

57. The classic study is Richard W. Bulliet, *Conversion to Islam in the Medieval Period: An Essay in Quantitative History* (Cambridge: Harvard University Press, 1979).

58. We may also note that the apologies examined above all pack a great deal of Christian doctrinal and moral teaching into a few pages, and may well also have served as a kind of emergency catechesis for under-catechized, wavering Christians.

59. I am grateful to participants at the "Christian Theology and Islam" conference for

In any event—and I think this point is important—we must keep in mind that the preserved Arabic writings of thinkers such as Theodore, Habib, and 'Ammar should not be seen as works of systematic theology, but rather, to a large extent, as collections of apologetic arguments deemed *useful* in the sometimes desperate work of community preservation. Whether or not they form a consistent set of arguments is quite another matter, perhaps one about which these apologists were not overly concerned.

5. Apologetic Portfolios

I would like to suggest, then, that we think of the existing collections of Theodore's, Habib's, or 'Ammar's writings as—at least to a large extent—"apologetic portfolios," that is, as collections of *ad hoc* arguments that had proved their worth in actual conversation. This may have some implications for the study of their thought. To illustrate what I mean, let me suggest some metaphors that help explain the *role* that apologetic arguments played in their communities. For example, we could think of the apologists as guards, and their arguments as a defensive wall, set up around the Christian flock in order to resist attacks, but perhaps first and foremost to keep the sheep from straying outside of the fold. Or, changing the focus from those inside to those outside the wall, we may perhaps think of the apologetic arguments as *openings* in the wall around the Christian enclosure, where outsiders might be able to approach, peer in, and get some sense of the beauty to be found inside.[60] However we tweak the metaphor, the apologetic arguments mark the *perimeter*; the discourse *inside*—the richly textured biblical and patristic worldview of the theologian and his community—is often implicit or alluded to lightly in the apologetic arguments themselves. Occasionally, that worldview is put on display in collections of Old Testament *testimonia* or in discussions of liturgical practice—but that is a topic for another paper.[61]

---

conversation about these matters.

60. I make use of a metaphor like this second one in Mark Swanson, "Beyond Prooftexting (2): The Use of the Bible in Some Early Arabic Christian Apologies," in *The Bible in Arab Christianity*, ed. David Thomas, HCMR 6 (Leiden: Brill, 2007) 91–112, here 108.

61. With regard to Old Testament *testimonia*, see the article mentioned in the previous note. With regard to matters of prayer and the liturgy, see, for example, Theodore's *Chapters on Prostration to the Icons*, especially the climactic ch. 24 on the necessity of venerating the icon of the crucified Christ; Dick, *Traité du culte des icons*, 212–18, English translation in Griffith, *A Treatise on the Veneration of the Holy Icons*.

Lessons for Today?

It is, of course, not a straightforward matter to move from a set of medieval texts to "lessons" for Christians today. Still, a couple of comments may be useful.

In the first place, the arguments of Theodore, Habib, and 'Ammar that have been surveyed here were undoubtedly a salutary reminder to their readers—and may be also to *us*—of the genuine oddity of Christian belief. It is a great temptation for Christians, gathering together in Christian spaces and institutions—and often in the *absence* of people of other faith traditions—to regard Christian doctrine as something quite obvious. How could anyone actually believe otherwise? As an antidote to this, we Christian theologians *need* the questions from outside the assembly: "What do you *mean* by the Trinity of God?" "Why do you worship a crucified man?" And so on. It is a gift of the religious Other to make the familiar again strange, and in these texts of the True Religion apology, forged in long experience of conversation with Muslims, Theodore, Habib, and 'Ammar have distilled that gift to a terrific degree of potency. Christian teachings are *not* easy and familiar; they do *not* ooze elegance and refinement; they do *not* conform readily to what we observe in the world. We are reminded that faith is not our intellectual achievement, but God's extraordinary gift. We are reminded of our need for humility.

In the second place, the True Religion apology allowed Theodore, Habib, and 'Ammar to say something about what it means for Christians to live according to Christian teachings, that is, to embody the commitments they espouse—a theme that runs through a number of the contributions in this volume. The Christian life, they remind us, has a particular shape: not of reliance on violence, but of turning the other cheek; not the pursuit of wealth and status, but of self-giving and contentment; not of license, but of discipline of the appetites; not of zeal for tribe, but of embrace of all nations.

And finally, Theodore, Habib, and 'Ammar suggest a way for Christian theologians to think about the encounter with Islam: not as something to be evaded, but also not as a systematic enterprise. Rather, Theodore, Habib, and 'Ammar are models of theologians who have ears wide open to Muslims' speech, questions, and concerns—and who take advantage of opportunities for conversation, engagement, and explanation as they arise.

4

Christian Theology in Conversation with Judaism and Islam

How Theologians of the Period Engaged with Non-Christian Sources and Traditions

David B. Burrell, CSC

None of the traditions that we have come to call (with Louis Massignon) "Abrahamic faiths" enjoyed in medieval times an overarching polity that gave them all space for "freedom of worship" as we recognize that practice. That has been, as we all recognize, one of the fringe benefits of a "secular polity," whatever meanings ensuing practices have come to bestow upon that term. Indeed, the environment closest to what we enjoy would have obtained under Islamic polities faithful to the Qur'an's injunctions regarding "no compulsion in religion," together with the tolerant verses regarding "peoples of the Book." And few polities designed to promote a milieu favorable to a particular revelation have been able to be faithful to that revelation, for fear that it might restrict the hegemony of the religious tradition charged with promoting the revelation. So whatever "conversations" might have obtained were inevitably overshadowed by power relations, where either Christians or Muslims dominated, while Jews would be the ubiquitous and presumed minority in either society. So while *disputations* might be considered *conversations*—in the operative sense that wrangling between persons or among groups is better than ignoring each other—I have chosen to give scant mention to the regular practice of disputations in either Christian or Islamic society. These exchanges have been treated extensively by people instructed in such matters (Gabriel Reynolds 2004), nor does there seem to have been much mutual profit from them beyond confirming stereotypes—if one can call that profitable at all! So to find conversation with intellectual fruit, one must look to the ways in which scholars of these respective communities sought assistance from each other in expounding truths central to each Abrahamic faith—notably, that of free creation—in the face of a pervasive set of philosophical convictions to the contrary. Yet serendipitously, that same philosophical culture provided strategies assisting persons of disparate faith convictions to converse with one another in a discourse, shareing the common presumption that "truth is where one finds it." So "philosophy"—a Hellenic import into each of the religious cultures—could mean either a monolithic teaching that contradicted key premises of one's faith, or a set of available strategies to give coherent voice to that same faith. And each of these traditions will have advocates promoting one *ethos* or the other, yet those who approached it constructively found themselves in conversation with persons of "other faiths," so the catalyst of philosophy will prove critical to our exposition.

A shared philosophical matrix offered medieval thinkers a context not unlike what the sea change effected in Vatican Council II offers to a Christian understanding of and relation to "other religions." Though our brief is the medieval period, some grasp of the new context in which we operate may help spare our accounts of medieval exchanges from anachronism. Indeed, we are familiar with the way Christianity commonly presumed the "new covenant" to have eclipsed the "old," if not in its official doctrines, certainly in the thrust of patristic writing, and in ongoing relations with Jews in their midst. And when it came to Islam, the very thought of a "new revelation" to a prophet in seventh-century Arabia could only be oxymoronic for Christians, who considered their "new covenant" to definitively preclude any fresh revelation after the death of John the evangelist. So using the only category available for grasping the set of portentous events that ensued from the seventh century on, Islam would at best be identified as a "Christian heresy." The most succinct presentation of the sea change initiated by the Vatican II document *Nostra Aetate* can be found in Karl Rahner's "world-church" essay, originally published as "Towards a Fundamental Interpretation of Vatican II" and variously reprinted (Rahner 1979). He has recourse to a fresh periodization of Western Christian history to attempt to explain what happened in regard to the church's attitude toward "other religions" in Vatican Council II. To paraphrase, with observations of my own, the major documents of Vatican II had already been presaged by developments in European Catholic thought in the preceding decades, usually referred to as "la nouvelle théologie" with the overriding slogan of "resourcement." Yet two slim documents—*Nostra Aetate* and *Dignitatis Humanae*—were to emerge from the council itself, in response to developments in the surrounding culture, the latter regarding freedom of religion in human society, largely attributed to the work of John Courtney Murray, SJ, regarding American Catholic experience.

In an effort to render a fresh start in interfaith attitudes plausible, Rahner introduces the notion of a "theological crisis," offering a fresh periodization of Western Christian history to illuminate the crisis that elicited *Nostra Aetate*, namely, that we are asked to address an issue for which there is little or no available theological reflection. To make his point, he suggests paralleling 70 C.E. with 1970 C.E., thereby bracketing nineteen centuries of Western Christian history, labeling it "Western European Christianity," including the missionary movement under this umbrella. The Christian community was faced, both in 70 C.E. and in 1970 C.E., with a "theological crisis" that demanded a decision without antecedent theological reflection. In 70, the issue was whether Gentile converts were to be circumcised or not. One could certainly have developed an argument in favor of the practice, citing the way "ontogeny reflects phylogeny," thereby dramatically reminding each male convert to Christianity of its Jewish provenance. Yet Paul's practice, with the community's decision (Acts 15), moved sharply against circumcision for Gentile converts to the faith. Rahner associates this communal action with the symbolic date of 70 C.E., the Roman destruction of the temple in Jerusalem, long taken by Christians to be a public divine sign that the new covenant had replaced the old. Indeed, until *Nostra Aetate*, that had been the overriding conviction of Christians regarding Jews in their midst. For Rahner, deliberations regarding that document displayed a fresh "theological crisis," for beyond a few pioneers, there had been little reflection on the relation of Christianity to "other religions," and the practices of the "missionary movement" generally reflected those of Western colonialism, with a few notable exceptions. Yet by Vatican II, cultural changes had so altered the landscape that the voices of these pioneers and exceptions were poised to win the day. Rahner lists a few such changes, beginning with decolonization in the wake of World War II, Paul VI's initiative to promote indigenous Catholic hierarchy in postcolonial lands, the way liturgical reforms preceding the Council decentered Catholic worship from Latin to vernacular languages, and finally, the United Nations General Assembly phenomenon relegating Europe and North America to a minority position. However cumulative these reasons proved to be, they were effectively catalyzed by the Nazi attempt, under the cover of the war, to exterminate Jews simply because they were Jews, forcing a reassessment of Christian attitudes toward the "other" in their midst, then extended to the more antagonistic "other" of Islam as well.

Rahner's attempt to make it plausible reflects the effect of this sea change on all Christian groups, with the exception of those unable to embrace God's universal salvific will of for all humankind. Though this had long been a standing teaching of the "great church," however muted in different times and places, it was roundly reaffirmed in Vatican II's Dogmatic Constitution on the Church, *Lumen gentium* (DiNoia 1992). So the issue we are considering—Christian theology in conversation with Judaism and Islam—can be considered without making "salvation of other-believers" its centerpiece. Indeed, I would argue that it must be considered apart from that neuralgic issue, for if truth be told, salvation is God's business, not ours. What the Council of Trent insisted upon for "same-believers"—"It is impossible, without a special revelation, to know whom God has chosen as His own"—must be true *a fortiori* for "other-believers" as well (Denzinger 1973, 805). What is rather at issue is the inherent role such "conversations" play in leading each of the interlocutors into a more profound understanding of the revelation they have received, have worked to expound, and try to live by. Medieval examples of exchange, and of the mutual illumination that results, offer a good starting point, which can be expanded with some salient early modern examples, until we encounter the pioneers who influenced *Nostra Aetate*, which will bring us to the flourishing evident in our day.

Medieval Exchange

The metaphysical challenge to Muslim, Jewish, and Christian thinkers turned on conceiving the One from whom all-that-is freely emanates. Even if *emanation* had to be rejected in the form that al-Farabi and Ibn Sina had proposed, using the logical model of necessary deduction, it remains the best corrective to the biblical metaphor of *artisan* in our attempt to capture the *sui generis* activity of creating (Burrell 1986). Hence Aquinas will not hesitate to characterize creation as the "emanation of all of being from the universal principle of all being" (*ST* 1.45.1), even after he has taken pains to follow the lead of Moses Maimonides to eviscerate any hint of logical necessity associated with *emanation*. In fact, by following the scriptures to rehabilitate the master metaphor of artisan, he prepared the way for depicting the act of creation as a free act of practical reason, so implicitly upsetting the predilection for speculative reason endemic to Hellenic thought (Burrell 1992). But how can we possibly understand the freedom peculiar to the One who creates without gaining anything from it? As Aquinas implied, in his pithy résumé of the Trinitarian structure inherent in creation properly conceived, the gracious move to creating a universe in the absence of any need whatsoever is best conceived as the One's acquiescing to the One's own inner constitution. What constitutes free creation, then, would be that gratuitous act of acquiescing, much as we consent to what we discern to be the good held out before us—whether it be spouse or vocation—in an act that is the very source of freedom without itself being a *choice* at all (Simon 1969).

The interactive culture of the twelfth to thirteenth centuries offers a window on Aquinas' creative transformations of Aristotelian *scientia*, as he sought to develop Augustine's prescient description of *theologia* as *fides quaerens intellectum*. Recent studies of Moses Maimonides—Faur, Kraemer, Seeskin, Stern, Davies—identify Maimonides' "method" as a *dialectical* pedagogy designed to help us appropriate the skills required to negotiate a quest for knowledge (*scientia*) within the ambit of *unknowing* fitting for human beings' attempts to understand divinity. What readers of Maimonides have identified as "esoteric" becomes for Aquinas the analogical use of language. Indeed, human language reaching for anything beyond the descriptive has always been pushed to metaphor and analogy. Just as, in practice, Aristotle's "scientific" inquiry was never deductive but inherently dialectical by testing distinctions in discourse, and seldom adhering to his own stringent norms in the *Posterior Analytic*, so Aquinas' desire to exhibit how *sacra doctrina* could be a way of knowing will studiously avoid a procrustean understanding of *scientia*.

His guide will be "Rabbi Moses," who felt the need to refine scriptural language to the point of resisting any straightforward assertions about divinity. Interestingly, Aquinas agrees with him on this, though he inherits semantic resources from twelfth-century Christian reflections on scriptural exegesis which will allow to him display how theological inquiry can effectively employ analogous terms, while confessing the "imperfect understanding" we inevitably have of them. This tension will be exhibited in the *manner* in which propositions are asserted, so displaying the quality of judgment needed to engage in this mode of knowing (*scientia divina*) (Venard 2002). And while Maimonides disavows what the Islamic philosophical tradition understood "analogous terms" to be, his practice again and again displays that quality of judgment needed to employ language properly in this arena of *unknowing*.

The key role played by Maimonides in fruitful intellectual exchange among Abrahamic believers is in part a function of available texts, yet also displays Maimonides' strategic placement "between the worlds," given Samuel Ibn Tibbon's contemporary translation of the *Guide of the Perplexed* into Hebrew. The rapid Latin rendering of that text for Aquinas complemented Avicenna's metaphysics rendered in Latin, though he only knew al-Ghazali by his "Intentions of the Philosophers," an adaptation of Avicenna's compendium in Persian, *Danesh Nameh*. As a result, Aquinas was never to taste Ghazali's more dialectical mode of inquiry into matters religious in his own "summa," *Ihya Ulum ad-din* ("Revivifying Religious Learning"). So Maimonides' *Guide*, attempting to conciliate reason with faith in a way similar to Aquinas' intent, became a key locus of Christian-Muslim encounter for both Aquinas and his teacher Albert, as Maimonides had effectively assimilated the Islamic philosophical tradition.

On a more strictly metaphysical level, the Arabic text *Kitab al-khair*, known in Latin translation as the *Liber de causis*, will offer both Albert and Aquinas a way of articulating the origination of all things from a creator, while each attempts to minimize any "necessary" connotations of the emanation doctrine articulated there. The imperative for a fresh conceptual strategy stems from the patent fact that none of Aristotle's celebrated "four causes" is adequate for the act of creation, since the most obvious candidate, *efficient cause*, could never act without a substratum on which to operate. The strategies of this Islamic recasting of Proclus will press Aquinas to a fresh understanding of Avicenna's "real distinction" between *essence* and *existing*, offering as it does a reflection of the creator in the created universe—albeit quite beyond any conceptual articulation.

Aquinas learned to use the *Kitab al-khair* (*Liber de causis*) in the following way, as displayed from his commentary (Gualiardo et al. 1996). The fullness of the act of existing is displayed in its very order, much as the efficacy of any of our actions is assured by its orderly advance toward its goal. We focus authentically on the action intended by aligning all the relevant features in a proper order, so that the effect is orchestrated. Notice that we cannot escape metaphors here, for there can be no ordering given. Revelation assists by allowing us to name "the Good," and also by providing us with some strategies of ordering—the Torah, the example of Jesus, the Qur'an—yet here again, discernment is always needed, and traditions can subvert as well as elaborate a given revelation. The ur-pattern derives from creation, as conceived by the *Liber de causis*: orderly emanation from the One so that the intentional portion of creation desires to return to its source. Yet here the order is not imposed but is inherent, as *existing* is not an added feature but an inherent gift. This is seen most fully, according to Aquinas, when we can appreciate this unitary source as freely bestowing on others what it is paradigmatically. And since its manner of being is triune, in creating it freely communicates the manner in which it naturally communicates (*ST* 1.32.1.3).

Now we can return to the original question: how is it that the One, whose proper effect is things' very being, effects that? The *Liber de causis* says, "first cause infuses all things with a single infusion, for it infuses things under the aspect [*sub rationem*] of the good" (123 [110]). Aquinas concurs, reminding us that it had already been shown that "the first cause acts through its being, . . . hence it does not act through any additional relation or disposition through which it would be adapted to and mixed with things" (123–24 [111]). Moreover, "because the first cause acts through its being, it must rule things in one manner, for it rules things according to the way it acts" (134 [111]). The following Proposition 21 links this "sufficiency of God to rule" (125 [112]) with divine simpleness: "since God is simple in the first and greatest degree as having his whole goodness in a oneness that is most perfect" (126 [113]). Hence Proposition 23 can assert, "what is essentially act and goodness, namely, God, essentially and originally communicates his goodness to things" (1342 [118]). With such a One there need be no anxiety about "control"; indeed, the simile that the proposition on divine rule elicits is that "it is proper for a ruler to lead those that are ruled to their appropriate end, which is the good" (ibid.). And to "infuse things under the aspect of the good" is precisely to bring all things to be in an order inherent in their very existing, so there is nothing "external" about divine providence, no imposition: neither "inasmuch as it establishes things, which is called creation; [nor] inasmuch as it rules things already established" (137 [122]). Indeed, initial diversity comes from the first cause, who "produces the diverse grades of things for the completion of the universe. But in the action of ruling, . . . the diversity of reception is according to the diversity of the recipients" (137 [123]). Yet since the original order comes from the One, the One in ruling will "effortlessly" adapt itself to the order established in creating. Another way of putting all this, and one that should dissolve most conundra regarding "divine action," is to remind oneself that the creator, in acting, acts always as creator; and this proposition elucidates Aquinas' contention that *creating* and *conserving* are the same action, differing only in that conserving presupposes things present.

Yet since the manner of that action will ever escape us, for its very simplicity belies any *manner* at all—no "relation or disposition" (Maimonides)—the best we can do is to remind ourselves that the creator always acts by constituting the order that inheres in each existing thing in the measure that it is what it is. (And since *essence* measures *esse*, it is pointless to oppose *essence* to *existing* in things that are.) Yet since "order" is a consummately analogous term, we can never be sure that we have detected the originating divine order in things, though our conviction that there is one, inscribed in their very being and our intentional attitudes toward them, will continue to fuel our inquiry. Crude classifications—inanimate, animate, intentional—can be supplemented by refined mathematical structures and symmetries (as in DNA), yet each set of analytic tools will be serving our innate desire to unveil the activity present in these infused "goodnesses" (130 [116]) that constitute our universe. And to grasp something of that constitutive ordering is to come closer to its source, "because every knowing substance, insofar as it has being more perfectly, knows both the first cause and the infusion of its goodness more perfectly, and the more it receives and knows this the more it takes delight in it, [so] it follows that the closer something is to the first cause the more it takes delight in it" (138 [123]). All is not light or delight, of course, because in truth we cannot, ourselves, hope to *know* "the first cause and the infusion of goodness." Indeed, "the most important thing we can know about the first cause is that it surpasses all our knowledge and power of expression" (46 [43]), for "our intellect can grasp only that which has a *quiddity* participating in 'to-be' [while] the *quiddity* of God is 'to-be itself'" (52 [17]). Indeed, that is why Aquinas can concur that "the first cause is above being inasmuch as it is itself infinite 'to-be'" (51 [47]). Yet since "what belong to higher things are present in lower things according to some kind of participation" (30 [17]), we can be said to share, as beings, in this inaccessible One.

We have seen how the imperious demand to *distinguish* creator from creatures dominates medieval philosophical theology, along with a semantics that will allow one to articulate divinity without *ipso facto* reducing it to something created. Here is where both Jewish and Muslim insistence on the *oneness* of God issues in semantic rules designed to keep divinity properly distinct from all that is created, so Christian philosophical theologians were beholden to Jewish and Islamic thinkers to thread their way in these arcane regions. What proves significant here is the way in which this presumption is shared by Jewish and Muslim thinkers as well. Without benefit of an explicitly Trinitarian revelation, both Moses Maimonides and al-Ghazali perceive clearly how the issue of free creation implies and is implied by the unanticipated and undeserved bestowal of the Torah and of the Qur'an, respectively. Indeed, it belongs to the ethos of Islam to insist that humankind needs to be alerted to the traces (*ayât*) of divine wisdom in the world by pondering the verses (*ayât*) of the Qur'an. One might indeed reason to the universe's origination, after the fashion of the Muslim *falâsifa* and in the spirit of Plotinus, but to see all-that-is as the "best possible" effect of divine wisdom requires God's revelatory initiative (Ormsby 1984, 1990). Yet once averred, the word of divine creative wisdom assumes center stage in creation. Here the testimony of revelation, as in the Qur'an's repeated avowal "God said 'be' and it is" (6.73), confirms the inference from metaphysics that creation involves no change at all (Aquinas, *ST* 1.45.2). In literary terms shared by both Bible and Qur'an, everything is accomplished by God's merely speaking the creative word, the Word that is made Arabic in the Qur'an and human in Jesus. And that same Word, "by whom the universe is made" (John 1:10), structures the very order of the universe, allowing the universe itself to disclose traces of divine wisdom to those attuned to it.

Here is where Aquinas' metaphysical theorem, enunciating creation by identifying created *esse* as a participation in the *esse subsistens* of God, joins the intentional discourse of *word* and *wisdom* to remind us how elusive must be the relation of creation to its creator. Kathryn Tanner (1988) has elaborated a set of semantic rules to articulate properly what she calls a "noncontrastive" relation of creatures to their intentional creator. The effort dovetails with Sokolowski's "distinction," as each reminds us that the creator cannot be "other than" creatures in the way in which one creature is other than another. Sara Grant (1991) carries this mode of thought a step further to make a highly suggestive connection with Sankara's *advaita*, proposing that we read Aquinas' determination that creation consists in a "nonreciprocal relation of dependence" in creatures as a Western attempt to articulate what Sankara calls "nonduality." For is that not what the "noncontrastive" relation between creator and creatures comes to, in our terms: not *other*, yet not the *same* either? So what has long been regarded as sharply differentiating Western from Eastern thought turns out to be a conceptual illusion on our part: did we think that we could adequately distinguish God from creatures to so readily accuse Hindu thought of failing to do so? Charges of "monism" came to abound; can they be sustained? We must also revise, as I have suggested, any sharp difference between emanation properly understood (that is, no longer identified with its model of logical inference) and free creation, perhaps coming to regard these two schemes as complementary ways of articulating what defies proper conceptualization. Here a study of Aquinas' dicta would have to be complemented by an examination of Meister Eckhart's assertions regarding these matters, allowing for a signal difference in the genre of their writings as well as the goal of their respective inquiries (Wendlinder 2004). Aquinas' goal was to show how and in what respect *theologia* could be a *scientia* (where both terms become ambiguous for modern readers when translated), while Eckhart, presuming that work had been accomplished, could focus on plumbing the implications of the teaching itself.

We have noticed suggestive affinities between our epoch and the medieval which historical scholarship regularly managed to avoid until recently: the interfaith dimension. It is significant that Aquinas turned to "Rabbi Moses" (who lived and worked in "the Islamicate" [Marshall Hodgson]) as a key interlocutor in developing his project of enlisting reason to elucidate faith, while Avicenna's distinction of *esse* from *essence*, suitably transformed, offered the tool he needed to appropriate Hellenic philosophy to his purposes. In that sense, the classical Christian synthesis begun with Albert yet wrought largely at the hands of Aquinas can be seen to have already been an intercultural, interfaith achievement. The relationship is more inherent and dialectical than it is one of traceable "influence," though Aquinas did read Maimonides' *Guide for the Perplexed* as soon as it was translated into Latin, and we can easily trace at least five central strategies that Aquinas adopted from him (Burrell, 1989). In the endeavor that Maimonides and Aquinas shared, al-Ghazali would have been a more relevant Islamic interlocutor than Ibn Sina, but the only work of his that Aquinas knew was the *Aims of the Philosophers*, which is little more than a recasting of Avicenna's summary of "philosophy" composed in Persian, the *Danesh Nameh* (Janssens 1986). So Aquinas never encountered his Islamic counterpart struggling with faith/reason issues the way Maimonides had, yet we can do so, and with great profit. In sum, the capacity to find analogies in the ways that thinkers from other faiths utilize reason to illuminate and critically appropriate their tradition can offer us a strategy for comparative understanding whose results are not unlike those claimed for "natural law"-type inquiries. Yet with the decided advantage that we need not claim anything more for "natural law" than the fact that the key notions in such questions prove to be inter-translatable in the minimal sense of providing fruitful comparisons.

A near contemporary of Thomas, his Dominican brother Riccoldo de Monte Croce (c. 1243–1320), was sent on mission to Baghdad from Florence. A pervasive Arabophilia suffused much of the Italian peninsula during the late thirteenth century. Interest in Arabic language, literature, philosophy, and science was evident in many places: from the university at Bologna, which became a center of Averroism, to the Sicily of Frederick II, an accomplished Arabist who employed a full-time court translator, and then to Florence itself, whose native son's *Divina Commedia* was clearly touched by Islamic literature. In a recent dissertation on Riccoldo, Rita George Tvrtković shows how his quite conventional opinions about Islam were constantly being modified by living among Muslims in Baghdad, to the point where he began to experience that "mutual illumination" that characterizes every boundary-crosser in religious domains (Tvrtković 2007). A slightly older contemporary of Riccoldo, Ramón Llull (1232–1315), authored more than two hundred works, established a college near his home in Majorca for training missionaries to Islam, and at the Council of Vienne (1311) elicited decrees to found schools of oriental studies in Paris, Oxford, Bologna, and Salamanca, where Arabic might be taught, together with the history, theology, and philosophy of Islam (Fletcher 2003).

From Early Modern Examples Up to the Present

The counterpoint to such fruitful medieval exchanges were, of course, the Crusades, yet even in the midst of war, interactions occur. By the fifteenth century, however, two figures emerge who initially collaborated in the Council of Basel, while each also searched for ways to engage Islam other than militarily: Juan de Segovia (d. 1458) and Nicholas of Cusa (1401–64). After the pointed controversies in the wake of Basel (and what became known as "conciliarism," an effort to restrain papal power), which drove a wedge between them, Juan spent what would be the last five years of his life in the village of Aiton, in the French Alps in the duchy of Savoy, where he received word of the fall of Constantinople to the Ottomans in 1453. This devastating news prompted him to dedicate his remaining years to promoting dialogue with Muslims as a strategy for achieving peace. He hoped to convert Muslims to Christianity, and his fellow Christians to a nonmilitary response to the events. Juan articulated these positions in several works that he sent to various contemporaries, in which he both recycles the rhetoric of an earlier era as well as approaches the issues from a new direction. At the same time, however, he welcomed the prominent Muslim jurist and scholar Yça Gebir (Gidelli) to his mountaintop priory, to help him produce a new translation of the Quran. This translation was trilingual (Arabic, Latin, Castilian), and while no longer extant, its fascinating prologue survived. Of course, encounters with Muslims in the Iberian Peninsula were more than just conversations among intellectuals who had never met any members of that faith tradition; they had a long history well before Juan de Segovia had been born. Segovia is a valuable case study of someone inheriting a tradition of discourse, with a trenchant European anti-Islamic rhetoric, yet reflecting on it via conversations with actual Muslims in Spain, and then adapting these reflections to the new Ottoman advances. He allows us to see how a fifteenth-century thinker adapted a discourse produced in an earlier era in different circumstances (Wolf 2003).

Juan's coworker, Nicholas of Cusa, was influenced early on by reading Ramón Llull, only to become cardinal archbishop of Brixen in the Tyrol. Yet when asked by his friend Aeneas Sylvius Piccolomini (Pope Pius II) to write in support of the latter's crusading plans, he produced *Cribratio Alcorani* ("The Sieving of the Qur'an"), arguing that if the Qur'an were intensively studied in the proper spirit ("sieved"), it would be found to be compatible with the teaching of Christianity as found in the New Testament. Beneath discrepancies and differences lay a shared basis of belief. In his most ambitious work, *Docta Ignorantia* ("On Learned Ignorance"), Nicholas went even further to insist on the inaccessibility of ultimate truth to the human intellect; wisdom lies in acknowledging ignorance (Miller 2003).

Napoleon's landing in Alexandria in 1799 signaled the onset of European colonizing activity in Asia and Africa, allowing firsthand exchange to replace romantic glimpses of Ottoman and Mogul life during the three previous centuries when Europe had been preoccupied exploiting two continents across the Atlantic. One to take full advantage of this new situation was Louis Massignon (1883–1957), a French Islamicist whose life and work was devoted to crossing boundaries, and whose dedication to the Muslim mystic and martyr al-Hallaj led him to "revert to faith in the God of Abraham" in such a way as always to think the revelations of Bible and Qur'an together (Gude 1995, Massignon 1982). We owe the prescient phrase "Abrahamic faiths" to Massignon, and there is little doubt that his longtime friendship with Pope Paul VI expedited the reconciling lines in the Vatican II document on the relation of the Catholic Church with other religions (*Nostra Aetate*). Blessed with a bevy of Muslim friends, plus fluency in Arabic, as well as enjoying a cultured family background and intellectual formation at the Sorbonne, Massignon's experience taught him that his Catholic faith cannot be "exclusive" in the sense of having nothing to learn from others. In fact, quite the opposite: encounter with persons of other faiths—in their case, Islam—invariably opens us to further reaches of our own. Indeed, it was Massignon's mysterious encounter with the subject of his study, Husayn ibn Mansur "al-Hallaj" (857–922), that allowed him to overcome nineteenth-century French intellectual prejudices against his ancestral Catholic faith. Massignon belonged to a burgeoning group of "Orientalists" in the early twentieth century, responding to the opportunities afforded them by European colonization. Yet Edward Said, critically identifying other Islamicists of the period, will find countless ways in which Massignon's work manages to elude the distorted construction of "Orientalist" he finds so offensive (Said 1978).

Interchange with Jewish scholars will have to wait until after *Nostra Aetate*—indeed, until a thriving cultural Judaism developed in Israel. *Nostra Aetate* stimulated Jewish-Christian dialogue, whose intellectual trajectory has been traced by two recent sets of essays by David Novak and Michael Wyschogrod, respectively, spanning the creative decades of this development (Novak 2005, Wyschogrod 2004, Burrell 2006). Through this conversation Christians discovered how inextricably Christian thought and worship is rooted in the Hebrew scriptures and subsequent Jewish practice, even while Christian tradition had early recourse to Hellenic philosophy to resolve central issues surrounding faith in Jesus as the revelation of God.

Conclusion

Faith as a Mode of Knowing in a Medieval and a Postmodern Interfaith Context

Even to suggest that faith and reason might complement one another in executing human inquiry is to move beyond the thought categories of modernism, where speaking of faith as a mode of knowing would have displayed a severe breach of etiquette, if not constituted an oxymoron. Alasdair MacIntyre's trenchant argumentation designed to show how any human inquiry must be tradition-directed recalls John Henry Newman's *Grammar of Assent*, composed to counter a set of Cartesian presumptions regarding paradigmatic rational inquiry in the heyday of modernity, the latter half of the nineteenth century (Lash 1983). The relevance of his reflective study today aptly confirms his observation that each idea has its proper context in time and place. Yet if the mutual normativity of faith and reason exemplifies the thirteenth century, while cleanly separating (if not opposing) them has characterized modernity, the move to postmodernity—however that protean term be construed—is intent (in its constructive mode) on seeking proper contexts for the exercise of reason. John Paul II's encyclical *Fides et Ratio* (*Faith and Reason*, 1998) illustrates this dynamic, even as the pope's offering faith as the fruitful context within which reason can flourish would have left Voltaire speechless. Yet the mode of reflection characteristic of Aquinas, with Jewish and Islamic luminaries, may well be poised to show us a way in which these two—faith and reason—are inextricably in need of one another. For that conviction suffuses their writings, while many things have conspired to bring us to a similar conviction in the wake of failed dichotomies that modernism presumed to be self-evident.

Bibliography

Burrell, David. 1982. "Why Not Pursue the Metaphor of Artisan and View God's Knowledge as Practical?" In *Neoplatonism and Jewish Thought*, edited by Lenn Evan Goodman, 207–16. Albany: State University of New York Press.

———. 1986. *Knowing the Unknowable God: Ibn-Sina, Maimonides, Aquinas*. Notre Dame: University of Notre Dame Press.

———. 2006. Review of *Talking with Christians: Musings of a Jewish Theologian*, by David Novak, and *Abraham's Promise: Judaism and Jewish-Christian Relations*, by Michael Wyschogrod. *Modern Theology* 22.4 (2006) 705–9.

Denzinger, H., editor. *Enchiridion Symbolorum*. Rome: Herder. #805; ET: *The Church Teaches*, ed. John Clarkson et al. St. Louis: Herder. #569.

DiNoia, J. A. 1992. *Diversity of Religions: A Theological Inquiry*. Washington, DC: Catholic University of America Press.

Fletcher, Richard. 2003. *Cross and Crescent*. New York: Penguin. 144.

Grant, Sara. 1991. *Towards an Alternative Theology: Confessions of a Non-Dualist Christian*. Bangalore: Asian Trading Corporation; 2002 edition by Bradley Malkovsky. Notre Dame: University of Notre Dame Press.

Gualiardo, Vincent 1996, with Charles Hess and Richard Taylor, translators. *St. Thomas Aquinas: Commentary on the Book of Causes*. Washington, DC: Catholic University of America Press.

Gude, Mary Louise. 1995. *Louis Massignon: The Crucible of Compassion*. Notre Dame: University of Notre Dame Press.

Janssens, Jules. 1986. "Le *Dânesh-Nâmeh* d'Ibn Sina: un texte a revoir?" *Bulletin de philosophie mediévale* 28 (1986)173–77; a more extensive study of "Al-Ghazzâlî and His Use of Avicennian Texts" has been published in the acts of the 1996 Budapest symposium on "Problems in Arabic Philosophy."

Massignon, Louis. 1982. *The Passion of al-Hallaj: Mystic and Martyr of Islam*. Translated by Herbert Mason. Princeton: Princeton University Press. Vol. 1, Foreword to the English edition, citation at xxv.

Miller, Clyde Lee. 2003. *Reading Cusanus: Metaphor and Dialectic in a Conjectural Universe*. Washington, DC: Catholic University of America Press.

Novak, David. 2005. *Talking with Christians: Musings of a Jewish Theologian*. Grand Rapids: Eerdmans.

Ormsby, Eric. 1984. *Theodicy in Islamic Thought: The Dispute over al-Ghazâlî's "Best of All Possible Worlds"*. Princeton: Princeton University Press.

———. 1990. "Creation in Time in Islamic Thought with Special Reference to al-Ghazali." In *God and Creation*, edited by David Burrell and Bernard McGinn, 246–64. Notre Dame: University of Notre Dame Press.

Rahner, Karl. 1979. *Theological Studies* 40 716–27; reprinted in *African Ecclesial Review* 22 (1980) 323–34.

Said, Edward. 1978. *Orientalism*. London: Routledge & Kegan Paul. 266–74.

Simon, Yves. 1969. *Freedom of Choice*. New York: Fordham University Press.

Tanner, Kathryn. 1988. *God and Creation in Christian Theology*. Oxford: Blackwell.

Tvrtković, Rita George. 2007. "The Ambivalence of Interreligiouis experience: Riccoldo da Monte Croce's Theology of Islam." PhD diss., University of Notre Dame.

Wendlinder, Anastasia. 2004. "Beyond Analogy: Articulating God's Transcendence and Immanence according to Thomas Aquinas and Meister Eckhart." PhD diss., University of Notre Dame.

Wolf, Anne Marie. 2003. "Juan de Segovia and Western Perspectives on Islam in the Fifteenth Century." PhD diss., University of Minnesota.

Wyschogrod, Michael. 2004. *Abraham's Promise: Judaism and Jewish-Christian Relations*. Grand Rapids: Eerdmans.

5

The Missing Peace of Evangelical Missiology

Peacemaking and Respectful Witness

Rick Love

CHRISTIAN-MUSLIM RELATIONS COMPRISE ONE of the momentous challenges of the twenty-first century.[1] The relationship between Christians and Muslims is supercharged by the "war on terror" and exacerbated by the fact that Western countries are perceived as "Christian" by many Muslims. On top of this, both Christianity and Islam are missionary religions, committed to sharing their faith with all peoples.

How then can followers of Christ be agents of peace and respectfully bear witness to their faith in a polarized and globalized world?

1. Evidence indicates that polarization between Christians and Muslims is increasing. A *Washington Post*/ABC News poll in 2006 found that nearly half of Americans have a negative view of Islam, a figure seven percentage points higher than it was a few months after September 11, 2001. Quoted in John Esposito and Dalia Mogahed, *Who Speaks for Islam? What a Billion Muslims Really Think* (New York: Gallup, 2007) 45.

Modern Evangelical missions have tended to focus on military metaphors and triumphal slogans to describe the church's global mandate.[2] These metaphors and slogans distort our mandate and negatively shape how we view the people to whom we are sent. In our zeal to fulfill the Great Commission, we have repeatedly misrepresented the way of the cross. We have often depersonalized the ministry of reconciliation. We have failed to model the peaceable way of Jesus.

I have served over twenty-five years among Muslims as an Evangelical. During this time I can remember only one person who shared with me the importance of an integrated approach to peacemaking and evangelism—David Shenk. (So I consider him one of my heroes and mentors.) I find biblical evidence of an integrated approach to peacemaking and evangelism to be rich and compelling. By contrast, I find a paucity of "peace" in Evangelical missiology (at least Evangelical praxis).

This isn't necessarily the case in other Christian traditions. I remember how I felt when I saw a political cartoon about Pope John Paul II on the Al Jazeera Web site. This Muslim Web site was famous for its political cartoons which strongly criticize leaders around the world, especially those in the West. But at the death of Pope John Paul II the cartoon was positive—depicting Pope John Paul II as a powerful spiritual leader dedicated to global peace. Tears welled up as I saw this poignant cartoon reflecting the spirit of the Prince of Peace.

One of my friends describes the impact of Pope John Paul II during his visit to a Muslim country.

> I recall when one small seismic shift took place. Pope John Paul II had chosen to visit our Muslim country on his tour, which would have almost gone unnoticed by me if it wasn't for the local reaction. I was sitting in the local café one morning when a friend of mine, a gentleman on the city council, asserted himself into my table and asked if I "had seen it." Seen what? The pope had spoken to over sixty thousand Muslims at the stadium the day before, but it was when the TV cameras picked up his arrival on the plane that this gentleman was rocked. The pope, he told me, had knelt and "kissed the ground." Kissed "our" ground. One small step for the papacy, one giant leap for ministry to Muslims!

2. See Rick Love, "Muslims and Military Metaphors," *Evangelical Missions Quarterly* 37 (2001) 65–68.

> The shift in attitude in my friend, in his understanding of a "Christian," had a positive impact that extended exponentially across that entire population.[3]

My experience and perhaps the perception of many Evangelicals is this: Peacemakers don't do evangelism and evangelists aren't known for being peacemakers. Peacemakers focus on social issues, while evangelists save souls. Peacemakers fear that evangelism among Muslims increases conflict, while evangelists believe that peacemakers compromise the gospel. Overstated? Yes. Stereotypes? Yes. But like all stereotypes, they reflect an element of truth. Most would agree that peacemaking and evangelism describe important biblical mandates, but rare is the church that practices both, and rarer still is the individual who practices both.

In this paper I want to examine the missing peace of evangelical missiology by tracing some of the fascinating connections between peacemaking and evangelism in the New Testament.[4] I hope to demonstrate the need for an integrated approach to peacemaking and evangelism that can be summarized as follows:

> There should be a strong congruity between our *message* (the gospel of peace), our *mandates* (peacemaking and evangelism), and our *manner* (the irenic way we carry out the Great Commission).

Because the challenge of peace between Muslims and Christians is one of the defining issues of this era, it is crucial that we understand and practice what the Bible teaches on this important topic.

This paper is exegetical and thus relates to any context. But I have written this primarily for those who work among Muslims. In order to demonstrate that an integrated approach to peacemaking and evangelism is possible, I will begin with a story.

The following story[5] illustrates how peacemaking and respectful witness have worked in a conflict zone. This story comes from Nigeria, where a

3. Brad Gill, "IJFM: Born to Be Wild?" *International Journal of Frontier Missiology* 25:1 (2008) 6.

4. The idea for the title of this paper came from Willard M. Swartley's excellent book *Covenant of Peace: The Missing Peace in New Testament Theology and Ethics* (Grand Rapids: Eerdmans, 2006).

5. This is a summary, with some direct quotations from Eliza Griswold, "God's Country," *The Atlantic*, March 2008, 40–55. The story of Pastor James and Imam Ashafa is also told in ch. 9 of *Peacemakers in Action: Profiles of Religion in Conflict Resolution*, ed. David Little (Cambridge: Cambridge University Press, 2007) 247–77.

Christian pastor named James and a Muslim imam named Ashafa founded the Interfaith Mediation Centre to bring about reconciliation and peace in Kaduna.

> *Pastor James was born in Kaduna. As a teenager James joined the Christian Association of Nigeria, and at twenty-seven became general secretary of the Youth Wing. When fighting between Christians and Muslims reached Kaduna in 1987, James became the head of a Christian militia. He used Scriptures to justify the violence.*
>
> *When James was thirty-two, a fight broke out between Christians and Muslims over control of a market. The Christians were outnumbered, and twenty of them were killed. James passed out, and when he woke up he found that his right arm had been sliced off with a machete.*
>
> *Imam Ashafa comes from a long line of Muslim scholars. In 1987, when religious violence hit Kaduna, Ashafa, like James, became a militia leader. He says, "We planted the seed of genocide, and we used the scripture to do that . . . as a leader, you create a scenario where this is the only interpretation." But Ashafa's mentor, a Sufi hermit, tried to warn the young man away from violence.*
>
> *"In 1992, Christian militiamen stabbed the hermit to death and threw his body down a well. Ashafa's only mission became revenge: he was going to kill James. Then, one Friday during a sermon, Ashafa's imam told the story of when the Prophet Muhammad had gone to preach at Ta'if, a town about seventy miles southeast of Mecca. Bleeding after being stoned and cast out of town, Muhammad was visited by an angel who asked if he'd like those who mistreated him to be destroyed. Muhammad said no. 'The imam was talking directly to me,' Ashafa said. During the sermon, he began to cry. Next time he met James, he'd forgiven him entirely. To prove it, he went to visit James's sick mother in the hospital.*
>
> *"Slowly the pastor and imam began to work together, but James was leery. 'Ashafa carries the psychological mark. I carry the physical and psychological mark,' he said.*
>
> *"At a Christian conference in Nigeria . . . a fellow pastor pulled James aside and said, in almost the same words as the Sufi hermit, 'You can't preach Jesus with hate in your heart.' James said, 'That was my real turning point. I came back totally deprogrammed.'*
>
> *"For more than a decade now, James and Ashafa have traveled to Nigerian cities and to other countries where Christians and Muslims are fighting. They tell their stories of how they manipulated religious texts to get young people into the streets to shed blood. Both still*

> *adhere strictly to the scripture; they just read it more deeply and emphasize different verses."*
>
> *Sadly, "the imam is frequently accused of being a sellout because he associates with Christians. He identifies himself very much as a fundamentalist and sees himself as one who emulates Muhammad. Although he and Pastor James don't discuss it, he also proselytizes among Christians. 'I want James to die as a Muslim, and he wants me to die as a Christian. My Islam is proselytizing. It's about bringing the whole world to Islam.'"*
>
> *"Such missionary zeal drives both men, infusing their struggle to rise above their history of conflict. . . . [Pastor James] still believes strongly in absolute and exclusive salvation mandated by the gospel: 'Jesus said, "I am the way and the truth and the life."' He still challenges Christians to rely on the strict and literal word, and he's still uncompromising on fundamental issues of Christianity."*

Please note: both Pastor James and Imam Ashafa engaged in peacemaking and respectful witness! In a conflict zone, the Muslim carried out *da'wa* (the Arabic term for Muslim outreach), while the Christian evangelized—and yet they remained friends and worked together for peace. Peacemaking and evangelism are not mutually exclusive!

Now let's look at the biblical evidence for an integrated approach to peacemaking and evangelism.

Peacemaking

The biblical magna carta of peacemaking is found in the Sermon on the Mount: "Blessed are the peacemakers, for they will be called the sons of God" (Matt 5:9).

Please note that this verse does not talk about "peaceful, peace-keepers, or peace-loving" people. In fact, it has nothing to do with personality types. It talks about people who defuse hostility and build bridges, people who resolve conflict and seek concord, people who call warring parties to peace, work toward the end of alienation, and pull down walls of hostility

Thus, I believe the New Living Translation best captures the intent of Matt 5:9: "God blesses those who work for peace, for they will be called the children of God."

In contrast to the other beatitudes, the term *peacemaker* describes an assertive action rather than a mere spiritual attitude. Thus, even the brash prophet John the Baptist could rightfully be described as a peacemaker.

God raised him up to "turn the hearts of the fathers to their children" (Luke 1:17) and "to guide our feet in the path of peace" (Luke 1:79).

The context of Jesus' ministry provides an important insight into the meaning of peacemaking. Jesus lived under Roman rule, ministering in an occupied territory. In the original context of the beatitudes, this emphasis on peacemaking was most likely directed against the Zealots, Jewish revolutionaries who hoped to throw off the yoke of Roman oppression and to establish the kingdom of God through violence. In contrast to the Zealots, Jesus speaks of a peaceable kingdom and a nonviolent extension of that kingdom.

The theme of peacemaking—if not the term—pervades the Sermon on the Mount. In fact, Glen Stassen, professor of ethics at Fuller Theological Seminary, considers the Sermon on the Mount "the *locus classicus* for Christian peacemaking."[6] Teaching on the following subjects directly relates to the tasks of peacemaking. To heed these topics is to follow the peaceable way of Jesus:

- Anger and reconciliation (5:21–26)
- Not resisting an evil person (5:38–42)
- Loving one's enemies (5:43–48)
- Forgiving (6:12, 14, 15)
- Not judging others (7:1–5)

The immediate context of this beatitude focuses on the social dimensions of peacemaking among friends, family, and community. But since Jesus mentions no qualifications to the nature of peacemaking, nor limits to the scope of peacemaking, it certainly relates to global challenges such as racism, poverty, and war as well. We should interpret peacemaking as broadly as the Bible does.

Jesus' use of the terms *opponent* (5:42), *Gentiles* (5:47; 6:7; 6:42), *enemies* (5:43–44), *unrighteous* (5:45), and *persecution* (5:10–12, 44) in the Sermon on the Mount indicate that peacemaking is not restricted to believers only. It takes place in an unbelieving world, beyond the boundaries of the church. Other passages in the New Testament confirm this. Paul urges the church in Rome thus: "If it is possible, as far as it depends on you, live at peace with everyone" (Rom 12:18, NIV). The author of Hebrews exhorts

6. *Just Peacemaking: Transforming Initiatives for Justice and Peace* (Louisville: Westminster John Knox, 1992) 37.

Christ's followers to "make every effort to live in peace with all (Heb 12:14, NIV). Children of God do peacemaking between believers *and* among unbelievers, both in the church and in the public arena.

Jesus describes peacemakers as blessed. This pronouncement of blessing expresses God's approval of those who work for peace. They are called children of God because they are acting like their Father, the God of Peace (Phil 4:9; 1 Thess 5:23) who sent the Prince of Peace (Isa 9:6) to bring about a world of peace (Luke 2:14).

P. S. Widjaja summarizes it well:

> We need to understand peace witness as a continuum, beginning from peace with God, moving into peace with ourselves, our families, our churches, those of other faiths, work colleagues, at the national and international level, and, most challengingly, with our enemies. Each Christian will be at a different point on the continuum, and must be encouraged to move on through it.[7]

Evangelism

The strong social dimension of peacemaking isn't all that's emphasized in the New Testament. There is also an evangelistic component. The gospel is the gospel of peace (Eph 2:13–17; 6:15). We have been entrusted with the ministry of reconciliation (2 Cor 5:19–21).We call people to peace with God (Acts 10:36; Rom 5:1).

Matthew 10 describes Jesus' commission of his disciples to extend the kingdom. In modern terms we would say that Jesus sent the apostles out on a "short-term missions trip." Jesus makes two references to peace in the context of evangelism. First, he tells the apostles how to discern the receptivity of people: "If the house is worthy, give it your blessing of peace. But if it is not worthy, take back your blessing of peace" (Matt 10:13, NAU). When Jesus sends out the seventy disciples (another "short-term mission"), he describes the process of discerning receptivity in a slightly different way: "Whatever house you enter, first say, 'Peace be to this house.' If a man of peace is there, your peace will rest on him; but if not, it will return to you" (Luke 10:5–6). This emphasis on the receptor's response to peace seems to be related to Jesus' promise a few verses later: "He who receives you receives Me, and he who receives Me receives Him who sent Me" (Matt 10:40).

7. P. S. Widjaja, "Peace," in *Dictionary of Mission Theology*, ed. John Corrie (Downers Grove, IL: InterVarsity) 280.

The concept of discerning and working with a man or woman of peace is a well-recognized missiological principle. People of peace become bridges to reach others because they respond to the gospel or because they at least support those sharing the gospel. What is not a well-recognized missiological principle is the spiritual dynamic of discerning the person of peace by imparting or withdrawing peace!

Most Western readers may see this as nothing more than a formality, a mere greeting (typical in the Jewish world, "shalom aleichem" and in the Muslim world, "as-salaam alaikum"). But Jesus' guidelines for these sent ones describe something more dynamic and spiritual than a greeting. According to New Testament scholar Donald Hagner, peace "is a benediction or blessing . . . which cannot ultimately be separated from the deeper sense of well-being associated with the gospel and its reception. The peace that the disciples can bestow is not available where the gospel and its messengers are rejected."[8]

This passage implies that in some sense those on mission are bearers of peace (cf. John 14:27), whose fruitfulness depends on the discernment of peace in evangelistic contexts.

While the practical implications of how to do this need to be verified through further experience and reflection, no one who takes Scripture seriously can doubt that peace is related to bearing witness.

The second mention of peace in Matthew 10 relates to persecution and suffering brought about because of fruitful evangelism:

> Do not suppose that I have come to bring peace to the earth. I did not come to bring peace, but a sword. For I have come to turn "a man against his father, a daughter against her mother, a daughter-in-law against her mother-in-law—a man's enemies will be the members of his own household." Anyone who loves his father or mother more than me is not worthy of me; anyone who loves his son or daughter more than me is not worthy of me; and anyone who does not take his cross and follow me is not worthy of me. (Matt 10:34–38, NIV)

Jesus' followers are peacemakers who speak the blessing of peace on families where they stay. Nevertheless, response to the message of the kingdom will be mixed; some will accept the message, others will reject it. Because of this, families will be divided and conflict will ensue. Jesus uses

8. Donald A. Hagner, *Matthew 1–13*, Word Biblical Commentary 33A (Dallas: Word, 1998). Electronic ed., Logos Library System S. 272.

the metaphor of the sword to describe the divisive fallout that sometimes accompanies the extension of the kingdom.

I am well acquainted with the painful consequences that can ensue because of the gospel. I have had friends who were renounced by their families because they were followers of Christ. I have had friends and acquaintances who were imprisoned and even martyred for the gospel. And I realize the greatest peacemaker who ever lived was crucified.

Among Evangelicals, Matt 10:34–38 (quoted above) rather than Matt 5:9 ("Blessed are the peacemakers") provides the dominant perspective regarding peace and evangelism in the New Testament. In other words, there is the assumption that conflict will prevail. With this mindset, could it be that conflict sometimes ensues because of the non-irenic manner in which we communicate the message? Could this be something of a self-fulfilling prophecy?

How do we reconcile Matt 10:34–38 with Matt 5:9? At the very least we need to affirm both truths, since the Bible does. Walter Kaiser gives wise guidance: "When Jesus said that he had come to bring 'not peace but a sword' he meant that this would be the *effect* of his coming, not that it was the *purpose* of his coming."[9] As children of God, our purpose is to represent the Prince of Peace, regardless of the effect it has.

The Great Commission in the Gospel of John provides another window into the relationship between peacemaking and evangelism.

> So when it was evening on that day, the first day of the week, and when the doors were shut where the disciples were, for fear of the Jews, Jesus came and stood in their midst and said to them, "*Peace be with you.*" And when He had said this, He showed them both His hands and His side. The disciples then rejoiced when they saw the Lord. So Jesus said to them again, "*Peace be with you*; as the Father has sent Me, I also send you." (John 20:19–21, my emphasis)

This passage describes Jesus' post-resurrection appearance to his disciples. He greets his followers with the standard Hebrew greeting: "Peace be with you." He then repeats this blessing of peace when he gives the Great Commission. Why the repetition? He seems to be hearkening back to his earlier promises of peace:

9. Walter Kaiser et al., *Hard Sayings of the Bible* (Downers Grove, IL: InterVarsity, 1997) 378.

> Peace I leave with you; my peace I give you. I do not give to you as the world gives. Do not let your hearts be troubled and do not be afraid. (John 14:27 NIV)

> I have told you these things, so that in me you may have peace. In this world you will have trouble. But take heart! I have overcome the world. (John 16:33 NIV)

These promises show the vital link between Jesus and peace: "*My peace* I give you," "so that *in me* you may have peace." They also show that peace is not the absence of anxiety or trouble. Rather, Jesus' peace enables us to remain calm and confident in the midst of conflict.

Therefore the blessing of peace becomes a key component of fulfilling the Great Commission.[10] The follower of Christ enjoys personal peace as he or she shares the gospel of peace. The media is the message!

The Gospel of Peace

The gospel itself expresses the integral relationship between peacemaking and evangelism. There are five texts in the New Testament that explicitly state or imply that the gospel is the gospel of peace (Acts 10:36; Rom 5:1–11; Eph 6:15; Eph 2:13–17; Col 1:15–20).

Acts 10:36

Luke summarizes Peter's ministry to the Roman centurion Cornelius in Acts 10. In the account of the Jewish apostle's first major outreach to the Gentiles, the content of the gospel is described as "peace": "You know the message God sent to the people of Israel, telling *the good news of peace* through Jesus Christ, who is Lord of all" (Acts 10:36, NIV, my emphasis).

10. "His words 'peace be with you' (repeated in 20:19 and 21) were a standard Hebrew greeting (Judg 6:23; 19:20; 1 Sam 25:6; 3 John 1:15), still used in the Middle East today. But here these words are far more than a greeting. At a profoundly personal level, Jesus is summing up the essence of his work and presence in the world. Peace is the gift of his kingdom. In 14:27 and 16:33 Jesus promised that this peace would be his gift to them; now he has delivered it." Gary M. Burge, "Jesus and the Upper Room (20:19–23)," in *John: From Biblical Text . . . to Contemporary Life*, NIV Application Commentary (Grand Rapids: Zondervan, 2000) 558.

The context implies that the good news about Jesus results in peace with God and peace between Jews and Gentiles.[11]

Romans 5:1–11

The second text about the gospel of peace is Romans 5:1–11 (only quoting the three most relevant verses 1, 9–11):

> Therefore, since we have been justified through faith, *we have peace with God through our Lord Jesus Christ* . . . Since we have now been justified by his blood, how much more shall we be saved from God's wrath through him! For if, when we were God's enemies, *we were reconciled to him through the death of his Son*, how much more, having been reconciled, shall we be saved through his life! Not only is this so, but we also rejoice in God through our Lord Jesus Christ, through whom we have now received reconciliation.

The good news of justification by faith results in peace with God—an objective peace with God (or status before God) established through faith in the death and resurrection of the Lord Jesus Christ. The nature of this objective peace is clarified in verse 9. Justification means that we are no longer threatened by God's wrath.

Paul then shifts from a legal metaphor (justification) to a relational metaphor (reconciliation) to give further understanding to the nature of this peace we enjoy. We are no longer God's enemies because we have been reconciled to God through Christ. The estrangement of sin and the resulting hostility have been dealt with on the cross, so our relationship with God has been restored. The peace of the gospel, then, includes both objective status and subjective experience.

There is no explicit social dimension to the gospel of peace in Romans 5:1–11. However, *inherent* in the gospel of reconciliation itself are massively important theological foundations for peacemaking. We were reconciled to God "while we were still helpless, ungodly, sinners and enemies" (Rom

11. "The author of Luke-Acts saw the word 'peace' as a capsule for that which the good news about Christ contains. It is incorrect to restrict the meaning to peace between God and humans . . . especially in this context of the gentile mission—where the universality of God's love and acceptance is being proclaimed—it is not irrelevant that one of the greatest human divisions of ancient society, that between Jew and gentile, is described as overcome. The similarities between this and Ephesians are worthy of note" (William Klassen, "Peace: New Testament," in David Noel Freedman, *The Anchor Bible Dictionary* [New York: Doubleday, 1992] 5:206).

5:6–10). God's love toward us is infinite and indiscriminate. This same kind of love enables us to embrace and make peace with the undeserving—including even our enemies.[12]

Ephesians 6:15

The next text describing the gospel of peace is found in the great spiritual warfare passage of Ephesians. Paul paradoxically speaks about peace in the midst of war: "and with your feet fitted with the readiness that comes from the *gospel of peace*" (Eph 6:15, NIV, my emphasis).

This piece of armor has to do with the Christian warrior's feet. The Roman *caliga*, a half boot used for long marches and studded with sharp nails for a firm grip,[13] is comparable to the cleats modern athletes wear in football, baseball, or soccer.

Admittedly there is some difficulty in interpreting this metaphor. The metaphor of boots could refer to *mobility* provided by the boots, in which case the focus would be on readiness to share the gospel of peace. Or the boots could refer to *stability*, in which case the focus would be on the peace the gospel gives the Christian under spiritual attack.

For both biblical and practical reasons, I would argue that the metaphor speaks of both mobility and stability.[14] The gospel of peace is a gift

12. For an excellent summary of this theme, see Miroslav Volf, "The Social Meaning of Reconciliation," *Interpretation* 54 (2000) 158–72.

13. Leon Morris, *Expository Reflections on the Letter to the Ephesians* (Grand Rapids: Baker, 1994).

14. It is difficult to decide between these two possibilities, since the text allows for either interpretation. "Readiness" to preach the gospel fits with the Old Testament background most likely shaping Paul's thought: "How lovely on the mountains are the feet of him who brings good news, who announces peace and brings good news of happiness, who announces salvation, and says to Zion, 'your God reigns!'" (Isa 52:7). Moreover, it fits best with the whole concept of spiritual warfare and evangelism as set forth by Paul: we preach the gospel "to open their eyes so that they may turn from darkness to light and from the dominion of Satan to God" (Acts 26:18). On the other hand, the more immediate context slightly favors the other interpretation. Paul mentions standing firm four times in this passage, which points toward an understanding of this verse in terms of stability.

In light of the rest of Scripture and the actual realities of spiritual warfare, I would say that both meanings must be emphasized. As Markus Barth has pointed out, these boots provided both stability and mobility; they gave Roman soldiers stability in combat and enabled them to go on long marches (*Ephesians* [Garden City, NY: Doubleday] 2:798; cf. Lincoln, *Ephesians*, 448). Thus, implicit in this metaphor is not only the image of a to be received and a message to be proclaimed. It must be appropriated personally and proclaimed publicly. Standing firm against the spiritual forces of darkness involves both experiencing the peace of the gospel and proclaiming the gospel of peace!

Ephesians 2:13–17

Evangelicals rightly focus on the *gospel of grace* as outlined in the first half of Ephesians chapter two (2:1–10). But too often the same focus is not given to the *gospel of peace* as outlined in the second half of Ephesians chapter two (2:11–22, esp. 13–17). Because of this, the traditional evangelical proclamation of the gospel has sometimes (often?) lacked social impact. But the same twofold emphasis on peace with God and peace between Jews and Gentiles asserted by the Apostle Peter in Acts 10:36 is also emphasized here by the Apostle Paul.

> But now in Christ Jesus you who formerly were far off have been brought near by the blood of Christ. For he himself is our *peace*, who has made the two one and has destroyed the barrier, the dividing wall of hostility, by abolishing in his flesh the law with its commandments and regulations. His purpose was to create in himself one new man out of the two, thus making *peace*, and in this one body to reconcile both of them to God through the cross, by which he put to death their hostility. He came and preached *peace* to you who were far away and *peace* to those who were near. (Eph 2:13–17, my emphasis)

Paul makes a number of stunning affirmations about the peacemaking work of Christ on the cross. First, *Christ's death has broken down every barrier* between Gentile and Jew. The "dividing wall of hostility" is a metaphor that probably refers to the wall that separated Jews and Gentiles in the temple. The "law of commandments" seems to refer to the strict dietary and cultic laws that kept Jews and Gentiles from social interaction. Many of these laws dealt with food, which means that the "table"—the place where people talk most personally and intimately over food—was not shared by Jews and Gentiles. Because of the death of Christ these Old Testament laws

---

defensive stance but also an offensive thrust. F. F. Bruce wisely summarizes: "Those who must at all costs stand their ground need to have secure footing; in the spiritual conflict, this is supplied by the gospel, appropriated and proclaimed" (*The Epistles to the Colossians, to Philemon and to the Ephesians* [Grand Rapids: Eerdmans, 1984] 408).

were no longer relevant to one's relationship to God. Table fellowship was established!

Second, Paul makes three positive affirmations about Jesus: *Jesus is our peace; Jesus makes peace; Jesus proclaims peace.*[15] These three affirmations dramatically underscore the reconciling purpose and unifying power of Jesus' person and Jesus' death.

Third, Ephesians 2:11–22 implies that *peacemaking should find embodiment in and through the church.* The two other references to peace in Ephesians further strengthen this view of the church as an instrument of peace (cf. Eph 4:3; 6:15). Andrew Lincoln summarizes well the practical implications of these profound truths:

> As the rest of the letter indicates, what has been achieved in the Church in the overcoming of the major division within humanity in the first century is an anticipation of God's purpose for the still-divided cosmos (cf. 1:10; 3:10). That major division can be seen as a prototype of all divisions (cf. Gal 3:28; Col 3:11). If the Church in Eph 2 stands for the overcoming of that fundamental division of humanity into either Jew or Gentile, it stands for the overcoming of all divisions caused by tradition, class, color, nation, or groups of nations. Anything less would be a denial of that nature of the Church which this writer takes as axiomatic.[16]

Colossians 1:19–20

The fifth and most comprehensive text on peace in the New Testament is found in Colossians 1:19–20:

> For God was pleased to have all his fullness dwell in him, and through him to reconcile to himself *all things*, whether things on earth or things in heaven, by *making peace* through his blood, shed on the cross.

15. Paul draws on Isaiah to explain the "peacemaking" nature of the cross. Most New Testament scholars note two key texts that Paul alludes to: "How lovely on the mountains are the feet of him who brings good news, who announces peace and brings good news of happiness, who announces salvation, and says to Zion, 'Your God reigns!'" (Isa 52:7); "'Peace, peace to him who is far and to him who is near,' says the LORD, 'and I will heal him'" (Isa 57:19).

16. *Ephesians*, Word Biblical Commentary 42 (Dallas: Word, 1990). Electronic ed., Logos Library System.

This is one of the most profound and astounding claims in Scripture! The gospel of peace has cosmic proportions—extending to both heavenly and earthly realities.[17] God's reconciling purpose at the cross is to restore the harmony of the original creation. The disharmonies of nature and the inhumanities amidst humankind will be put right.

These five texts describing the gospel of peace should significantly impact our approach to evangelism. Surely there should be congruity between our message and our missiology. Surely the message of peace should be communicated in an irenic manner worthy of this message!

Peacemaking among Jesus' Followers

I have had the privilege of studying under some of the best theologians and missiologists in America. I learned many valuable lessons about hermeneutics, biblical theology, strategy, culture, and contextualization. *Yet no one prepared me for the challenge of peacemaking* I faced as I confronted broken relationships in the church, on teams and in emerging churches around the world.

Yet the New Testament abounds with references to peacemaking for believers! For example, Paul addresses peacemaking in every one of his epistles, either through specific commands or concrete examples:

- "If possible, so far as it depends on you, be at peace with all men" (Rom 12:18).
- "So then we pursue the things which make for peace and the building up of one another" (Rom 14:19).
- 1 Corinthians 5: The whole chapter describes a peacemaking problem.
- "Finally, brethren, rejoice, be made complete, be comforted, be like-minded, live in peace; and the God of love and peace will be with you" (2 Cor 13:11).
- "Brethren, even if anyone is caught in any trespass, you who are spiritual, restore such a one in a spirit of gentleness; each one looking to yourself, so that you too will not be tempted" (Gal 6:1).

17. For an excellent summary of all the exegetical details, see Peter T. O'Brien, *Colossians-Philemon*, Word Biblical Commentary 44 (Dallas: Word, 1998). Electronic ed., Logos Library System S. 56.

- ". . . being diligent to preserve the unity of the Spirit in the bond of peace" (Eph 4:3).
- "I urge Euodia and I urge Syntyche to live in harmony in the Lord. Indeed, true companion, I ask you also to help these women who have shared my struggle in the cause of the gospel, together with Clement also and the rest of my fellow workers, whose names are in the book of life" (Phil 4:2–3).
- "Bear with each other and forgive whatever grievances you may have against one another. Forgive as the Lord forgave you. And over all these virtues put on love, which binds them all together in perfect unity. Let the peace of Christ rule in your hearts, since as members of one body you were called to peace. And be thankful" (Col 3:13–15, NIV).
- "Live in peace with one another" (1 Thess 5:13).
- "If anyone does not obey our instruction in this letter, take special note of that person and do not associate with him, so that he will be put to shame. Yet do not regard him as an enemy, but admonish him as a brother. Now may the Lord of peace Himself continually grant you peace in every circumstance. The Lord be with you all!" (2 Thess 3:14–16).
- "This command I entrust to you, Timothy, my son, in accordance with the prophecies previously made concerning you, that by them you fight the good fight, keeping faith and a good conscience, which some have rejected and suffered shipwreck in regard to their faith. Among these are Hymenaeus and Alexander, whom I have handed over to Satan, so that they will be taught not to blaspheme" (1 Tim 1:18–20).
- "Now flee from youthful lusts and pursue righteousness, faith, love and peace, with those who call on the Lord from a pure heart" (2 Tim 2:22).
- ". . . to malign no one, to be peaceable, gentle, showing every consideration for all men" (Titus 3:2).
- Philemon: The whole letter addresses a peacemaking situation.

According to Jesus, peace in the church has an important evangelistic impact. He makes this clear in his high priestly prayer: "I do not ask on behalf of these alone, but for those also who believe in Me through their word; that they may all be one; even as You, Father, are in Me and I in You, that they also may be in Us, *so that the world may believe that You sent Me*" (John 17:20–21, my emphasis).

This is one important aspect of the missing "peace" of Evangelical missiology![18]

Peacemaking and Respectful Witness

Evangelism should be carried out in a way that befits the gospel of peace and the mandate to work toward peace. Thus, it should be done in a positive, respectful way. A good example of this is Paul's approach to the Athenians in Acts 17.[19]

The idolatry of the Athenians incensed Paul's monotheistic heart: "His spirit was being provoked within him as he was observing the city full of idols" (Acts 17:16). Nevertheless, he demonstrated a respectful, gracious, and bridge-building approach to the Athenian heart. He affirms their religiosity (17:22), uses an altar as a point of contact (17:23), and quotes their own poets to help clarify the meaning of the good news (17:28).

But please note: to bear witness in a respectful manner does not mean that we cannot be bold in our proclamation. Paul was respectful and bold. He called the Athenians to repent because of coming judgment (17:30–31).

Last month I had the privilege of meeting with nine Egyptian sheikhs and two Syrian muftis. In both meetings, we discussed the importance of *da'wa* for Muslims and of evangelization for Christians. Both the Egyptians and the Syrians agreed that we must bear witness to our faiths, yet live in peace. One of the Egyptian sheiks said, "You must share your faith! But just don't attack Islam!"[20]

18. To help fill this gap, I wrote *Peacemaking: Resolving Conflict, Restoring and Building Harmony in Relationships* (Pasadena, CA: William Carey Library, 2000).

19 There is no mention of peace in this passage. However, it is noteworthy that Paul the apostle, "more than any other writer in the NT canon, makes peace, peacemaking and peace-building central to his theological reflection and moral admonition" (Swartley 2006, 190). As noted above, he describes the gospel as the gospel of peace four out of the five times it is described thus in the New Testament. In addition, the word *peace* is mentioned over forty times in his letters. Finally, more than any other New Testament author he refers to God as the "God of peace" (Rom 15:33; 16:20; 1 Cor 14:43; 2 Cor 13:11; Phil 4:9; 1 Thess 5:23; 2 Thess 3:16).

20. According to a recent Gallup poll, the majority of Muslims in the world believe that the West does not respect them. When asked what they admire least about the West, Muslims said, "hatred or degradation of Islam and Muslims" (Esposito and Mogahed, *Who Speaks for Islam?*, 61).

In the spirit of the Prince of Peace, respectful witness focuses on giving a positive presentation of the gospel, and it does not attack the other.

Peacemaking and Respectful Witness Revisited

This story comes from Indonesia, where a pastor and a commander of Hizbullah work together for peace.[21]

> *In 1998 serious conflict broke out between Christians and Muslims in the city of Solo, in Central Java. Consequently, the religious leaders formed an interreligious peace committee to rebuild trust and work toward concord. A young pastor on this committee tells of his first visit to the Hizbullah command center:*[22] *"The commander greeted him gruffly, 'You are a Christian and an infidel, and therefore I can kill you!' Unfazed, the pastor returned again and again to the commander's center to drink tea and converse."*
>
> *"Then the pastor invited the commander and his officers to fly with several Christian leaders to Banda Aceh to work with Christian teams in the post-tsunami reconstruction. . . . Remarkably, the Hizbullah leaders accepted, and for two weeks they worked with the Christian teams in rebuilding projects. The commander slept in the same room with the pastor, and they became friends! . . . He confided to the pastor, 'I have discovered that you Christians are good infidels.'"*
>
> *Afterwards they met again for further peacemaking talks. They had invited David Shenk to speak to the group and offered to translate the book he coauthored with Badru Kateregga titled* A Muslim and a Christian in Dialogue.[23] *When the pastor handed the book to the commander, he broke down: "When he regained his composure he said, 'I am overcome, for this book is revealing another way, the way of peacefully sharing faith instead of violently confronting one another.'"*
>
> *When asked about his evangelism, the pastor says, "'My calling is to bear witness, mostly through praxis, to the reconciling love of Christ. I give account of my faith in Jesus to all who ask. Conversion*

21. This is a summary, with some direct quotations from David Shenk, "The Gospel of Reconciliation within the Wrath of the Nations," *International Bulletin of Missionary Research* 32.1 (2008) 3–9.

22. Hizbullah means "party of God." This is not the same organization as the Shi'ite Hizbullah in Lebanon.

23. Badru D. Kateregga and David W. Shenk, *A Muslim and a Christian in Dialogue* (Scottdale, PA: Herald, 1997).

> *is not my responsibility; that is the work of God.' Remarkably his church has grown from 40 to 250 in the last dozen years, and with the advocacy of Hizbullah, they are planning to build a second church in Solo."*

Finding the Missing Peace for the Future of Evangelical Missiology

So how should the mandates of peacemaking and evangelism fit together? The biblical foundation laid in this study, along with the poignant stories from Nigeria and Indonesia, demonstrate that peacemaking and evangelism go hand and hand. There should be a congruity between our message (the gospel of peace), our mandates (peacemaking and evangelism), and our manner (the irenic way we carry out the Great Commission). We preach of peace, we work towards peace, and we imitate the Prince of Peace.

This approach to obeying Christ's last command elicits particular urgency since the challenge of peace between Muslims and Christians is one of the defining issues of this era.

The church should be a place where people study, practice, and proclaim peace. Moreover, the church's mandate to disciple all nations should be carried out in the spirit of the Prince of Peace—graciously and respectfully. May God raise up a new generation of peacemaking apostles.[24] If we seek the lost in this way, we will find the missing peace of Evangelical missiology!

24. I define an apostle as a cross-cultural disciple-maker serving in a pioneer context—a "sent one" who forms communities of Jesus' followers where Christ is not named (Rom 15:20).

6

In Search of New Approaches to Inter- and Intra-Religious Christian and Muslim Debates[1]

Nelly van Doorn-Harder

Introduction

CHRISTIANS AND MUSLIMS ALIKE agree that as our world is becoming more cosmopolitan, religious demographics everywhere are changing. In the United States, new immigration patterns that started during the 1960s have resulted in a religious landscape that is more pluralist than ever before. From the workplace to interreligious marriages, daily interactions have become more diverse than they were half a century ago, a reality that, according to Harvard scholar Diana Eck, has resulted in "an interfaith revolution."[1] A quick Google search confirms that this revolution has led to myriads of local, national, and international interreligious activities and networks.

Even those who think interfaith dialogues are futile agree that we can no longer afford to ignore the religious other. Whether our attitudes toward interfaith engagements range from apologetic to open-minded, from exclusive to inclusive, in our contemporary religious landscape both inter- and

1. [Ed.: notes for this chapter begin on page 120.]

intra-religious debates have become more important than ever. According to Robert Wilken, a "new kind of Christendom and a new kind of Islam" are emerging as both religions face the cultural and political challenges of the twenty-first century.[2] Vigorous inter- and intra-faith debates are being called for since they help shape new understandings of what religiosity means. In this new landscape, our internal debates are as important as our interfaith encounters, as the former sculpt our attitudes and thinking patterns toward those of other faiths. Thus, in order to create new religious and social spaces and alternative networks of engagement and solidarity, and serious interfaith interactions, Christian theologians need to go beyond the conventional models that have been practiced up until now.

This essay addresses the question of how we can find better models to strengthen the interfaith engagement and initiatives by reaching out to dialogue partners who seldom are included in conventional activities, as well as looking at some alternative practices. Although of global consequence, the majority of interfaith activities evolve from local, at times even personal, needs and circumstances. In order to show how local needs impact larger communities, I will highlight several projects developed in Indonesia, a Muslim majority country where groups of Muslims, Christians, Hindus, Buddhists, and Confucians cooperate to find new ways of interfaith engagement that directly or indirectly address social and religious problems within society.

Models of Interreligious Living

Examples in History

Religiously diverse societies are not exactly a new phenomenon. An often cited example is medieval Spain where between the eighth and fifteen century Jews, Christians, and Muslims lived together in relative harmony. As early as the third century BCE, King Ashoka expressed newfound Buddhist ideals in his Rock Edicts. Edict number VII stated that "all religious communities shall be able to reside everywhere," and in number XII the king wrote, "Whoever praises his own religion, due to excessive attachment, and denigrates that of others with the thought 'Let me glorify my own religion,' in reality inflicts the severest injury on his own religion. Contact therefore between religions is good: One should listen to and respect the doctrines professed by others and apply what one has learned."[3]

While the phenomenon of people of different faiths coexisting in the same space is not new, the social, political, and legal conditions under which groups found protection of their religious rights and freedom have changed profoundly since the fifteenth century. Since then, political and legal protection of communities has developed following three models that in part overlap. According to the first model, peace treaties allowed people of different religions to live in separate territories. This model developed in post-Reformation Europe and implied that, for example, Catholics living in Catholic territory had to move in the event that they became Protestant. The second model provided protection to religious minorities within a state in which an ethnic or religious majority ruled. An example of this model is the classical Islamic state which allowed its non-Muslim subjects to practice their religion in separation from the Muslim majority. The third and latest model follows universal human rights standards which should guarantee individuals freedom of religion or belief.[4]

Contemporary Notions

Many advocates of human rights consider the third model to be the most suitable for the twenty-first century. However, in many countries it is not fully applied or its conditions are broken when interreligious or interethnic violence erupts. This reality underscores the importance of the development of interfaith models that go beyond academic meetings or modes of living together, both of which lack concerted civil engagement efforts and exercises of learning and understanding.[5] Interfaith engagement, ideally speaking, functions as a tool for peacemaking and restoring broken communal relations. Ultimately the myriad of interfaith activities form the building blocks for the application of the fundamental right of freedom of religion. However, though most modern-day states in theory acknowledge this freedom, in practice its citizens might ignore it.

Art historian and theologian William Dyrness, inspired by the theories of Roberto Goizueta on religious participation, describes the current academic approaches to interfaith engagements thus: "We seek a better *understanding*, we promote inter-faith *dialogue*, or we exchange *ideas*—above all we give *papers*! One almost suspects that what is being promoted is a 'meeting of the minds' rather than of people."[6] In order to reach a level of true interaction and respect for each other's concerns, struggles, and plights, all people should be involved: not just men, but also women, children, and professional groups like artists. In human rights language, interfaith engagement can also be instrumental in promoting the rights of women and children. Involvement of different groups automatically implies that the scope of activities and issues covered will change.

Indonesia: The Bridge Building and Women Advocacy Projects

Having taught at a divinity school in Indonesia (1993–1999), I witnessed firsthand the necessity of interfaith engagements. Initiatives at the grassroots level proved especially vital when, after the fall of the repressive Suharto regime in 1998, relatively harmonious communal relationships broke down and resulted in nationwide incidences of violence. Several of the most successful projects were initiated by women and did not just focus on theological issues. Some projects were not considered to belong to interfaith engagement at all since they focused on one religion. Yet, because the outcome of their advocacy influenced the lives of many, they should be considered as contributions to the interfaith engagements.

With these considerations in mind, I chose two Indonesian initiatives as focal points for this essay. The first project is an interreligious initiative called the Bridge Building initiative titled "Globalization: Challenges and Opportunities for Religions." It was launched by the Center for Religious and Cross-cultural Studies (CRCS) and the Indonesian Consortium for Religious Studies (ICRS) at Gadjah Mada University (UGM) in Yogyakarta.[7] Both centers are dedicated to teaching and studying religions from an interfaith perspective, with both the students and staff representing most of the religions present in Indonesia (Islam, Christianity, Buddhism, Hinduism, and Confucianism). Their Bridge Building project aims at facilitating connections between peoples of different faiths who represent a wide spectrum of believers with various views on those of other faiths (and denominations). In a series of meetings the project brought together scholars, students, journalists, and activists belonging to radical, exclusive groups as well as those who were located on the inclusive, pluralist side of the religious spectrum. The second project is intra-Islamic and aims at addressing deeply engrained forms of injustice against women by probing the Islamic texts, heritage, and law in search of teachings that promote protection and respect for women. Both initiatives arose in the midst of growing influences of radical Islam in Indonesia, and both try to find ways out of a deadlock within the intra-Islamic and the interfaith engagements. Although very different from each other, they both go beyond the conventional interfaith agenda and share ambitious goals that seek to intervene in the current discourses and change the construction of ideologies about the religious other.

In summary, interfaith engagement is a complex activity that has become imperative in this period of globalization. There is much more at stake than just ideas, papers, and meeting of minds when communal relations break down or certain groups see their basic human rights taken away. For interfaith activities to be successful, in my view, intra- and inter-religious debates need to be held in tandem with a search for alternative models for interfaith engagement, especially now that these activities play a vital role in conflict meditation and the creation of true respect for the basic right of freedom of religion.

Modes of Interfaith Engagement

Unpredictable Influences

Several of the contributions in this volume relate how medieval Christian theologians crafted intricate apologetics to counter Islamic accusations concerning their belief in three gods and an incomprehensible Trinity. As Mark Swanson's article shows, the main goal of these theologians was to protect and preserve a fragile community that found itself under pressure from pro-conversion policies of the Abbassid rulers. What we can learn from these examples is that in the end many of the well-developed arguments were overruled, not by impressive theological or philosophical retorts but by external circumstances and events on the ground. The sobering realization that in the medieval Middle East external conditions caused many Christians to accept Islam reminds us of the reality that ingenious and convincing arguments presented by theologians and philosophers can often be shattered by a single social, economic, or natural event. In 1347, for example, the bubonic plague decimated the Coptic Christian community, while a few years later the policies of the Mamluk dynasty aimed at creating an Islamic civil society, which complicated the daily life of non-Muslims with anti-Christian riots and rules to enforce Islamic codes and behavior.

Many of the mechanisms we observe in the medieval situation still hold true today. The first is that up to today interfaith, or in this context specifically Muslim-Christian, relations still remain the purview of a relatively small group of scholars and practitioners whose sophisticated theological arguments seldom touch the lives of those at the grassroots level. Secondly, promising initiatives can either be shut down or catalyzed by external influences. The two Indonesian projects featured in this essay are examples of this reality. Thirdly, the medieval contributions are entirely theological and produced by men. Looking through the lens of theology only often leaves out the voices and contributions of women who, especially after occurrences such as natural or social disasters, are deeply engaged in interactions between various communities. Furthermore, it is easily overlooked that the theoretical dialogue omits discussions about the forces and realities that influence the daily lives of women. For example, limits set on Muslim women by the injunctions of Islamic law are seldom featured in academic interfaith meetings.

This essay does not make a case for abolishing the theological discussions. On the contrary, serious interfaith engagements are founded on systematic theological reflection, both Christian and Muslim. However, interreligious discussions within the two religions vary greatly. Leaving aside insoluble issues such as the Trinity and Jesus' divine nature, the way Christians and Muslims theologize differs greatly, especially in the treatment of law and tradition. In both religions, these deliberations tend to be the purview of men and frequently leave out important actors such as women and youth. By nature theology is not a discipline that yields immediate and tangible results; it often lags behind the facts, and the interfaith activities it engenders elicit criticism of being exercises in treading water.

Inclusive and Exclusive Views within Islam and Christianity

Although few Christians are aware of developments within Islamic theology, both religions face similar obstacles. The choice of the two projects highlighted in this essay is informed by this reality. The Bridge Building interfaith initiative was launched by several Muslim and Christian scholars who were united in their concern over pervasive trends of radicalism and fundamentalism within their respective religions. Within both religions, scholars and activists probe the holy texts for teachings that agree with a more open attitude toward those of other faiths and debate about how their beliefs inform opinions on issues that affect all of humanity, such as global warming. Most of these developments and discussions within Islam remain under the radar of the majority of non-Muslims. In the news, violence reigns, and thoughtful writings and documentaries that try to counter this prevalent focus on violence tend to be drowned out. Muslims all over the world are increasingly frustrated when vocal, intolerant groups shape the image of their religion. In fact, a fierce battle is being waged around the question of who has the authority to speak for Islam.[8] Needless to say, radical ideology within religions can have significant repercussions for interfaith encounters and for the position of religious minorities in Islamic countries.

In the search for correlations with other religions, balancing between openness toward the other and commitment toward one's own beliefs, Christian theologians have attempted to create a dialogical form of theology in which they interpret their own scriptures in view of the current-day religious plurality. Especially since the Second World War, they have discussed this reality since, up to the 1960s, most Christian approaches to interfaith dialogue were colored by missionary intentions of conversion. The watershed event showing that this attitude was changing came during the Second Vatican Council (1962–1965) when the Catholic Church issued the *Nostra Aetate* declaration, which urged Catholics to improve relationships with Muslims for the promotion of peace and social justice and stressed the spiritual patrimony it shared with Jews.[9]

In 1971 Protestants, united in the World Council of Churches (WCC), followed suite, forming a subunit to promote dialogue between people of living faiths that went on to produce a document called "Guidelines on Dialogue with People of Living Faiths and Ideologies." Documents calling its members to reflection and action followed at a steady pace.[10]

Declarations and activities from official church bodies resulted in scores of books exploring the level of commitments religious groups wanted to have in interacting with others.[11] Theologians explored reformulations of the Christian stances toward other religions in a pluralist context, stirring up intense discussions. The British theologian and philosopher John Hick developed a philosophy according to which the transcendent characteristics of religions derive from the same reality. With Leonard Swidler and Wilfred Cantwell Smith, he believes in a common basis for a value system that leads to a universal theology of religions.[12] In the United States, Catholic theologian Paul Knitter emphasized the ethical praxis of justice as a starting point for encounter with other religions.[13]

Several scholars have explored these opinions and concluded that true interfaith engagement via exclusive theological discussions is impossible. Catherine Cornille, for example, considers practicing the virtues of humility, commitment, interconnection, empathy, and hospitality to be a more fruitful basis for this engagement.[14] Convinced that a strong spiritual life allows us to be open to new experiences, Ursula King stresses the importance of the spiritual interfaith dialogue.[15] Paul Griffiths has argued that interfaith activities seldom involve rigorous intellectual sparring; its participants tend to stress similarities, ignore differences, and avoid deep-seated problems such as differences in respective religious experiences and truth claims. In his view, in order to avoid pointless polite talks, we need vigorous polemics.[16]

Griffiths' view relates to some of the responses that inclusive interpretations have elicited from those who stress or try to redefine the uniqueness of Christianity. Some emphasize the incommensurability of religions due to the reality that they represent different semiotic worlds. Others criticize trends of modernity, fearing that these could result in an amorphous religious mass. In many instances there is a fear that openness will result in the formation of one meta-religion in which not one specific religion finds preference.[17]

Among Muslims, we likewise see a range of opinions, from those arguing that there is no salvation outside Islam to those who believe that all religions can be a path to God. Fatimah Husein, who teaches at the State Islamic University in Yogyakarta, provides a theoretical framework for what constitutes exclusive and inclusive attitudes among Indonesian Muslims. According to her analysis, exclusivists apply a literal reading of the Qur'an and Sunna within a fixed interpretative framework that is past-oriented. They hold that salvation can only be achieved through Islam, are against a division between religion and state, and vie for the national application of the Islamic law, the Shari'ah, which they consider to be universal and regulatory of all aspects of life. Moreover, they believe in the existence of a global conspiracy against Islam. Muslims with inclusive religious views read the Qur'an contextually and advocate continuous reinterpretation. They hold that Islam is the best religion *for them* (unlike pluralists who believe all religions to be the same), argue for the separation of religion and state, and cherish the Shari'ah as a moral guidance.[18]

In the political arena, the contrasting views on the divine law of Shari'ah and its corollary of Islamic jurisprudence (*fiqh*) emerge as the most salient dividers between exclusive and inclusive attitudes. Many views and discourses on non-Muslims, who according to traditional legal rules belong to a well-defined category within Islamic society, are based on conventional jurisprudence. For example, Islamic law and jurisprudence not only provide rules for legal contracts such as marriage between Muslims and non-Muslims, but also for questions on mixed prayers and whether or not a non-Muslim is allowed to touch the holy Qur'an as well.[19] In Islamic discourse, theology and law are joined. Many Muslims assume that the legal system is unified and static, although in reality it is a product of human interpretation and application that can be adapted to the needs of the time.

The intra-Muslim discussions thus not only cover the Qur'anic injunctions concerning non-Muslims, but also include vigorous debates about the role and place of the Shari'ah and fiqh in personal life and society. In many countries Muslims are calling for the application of the Islamic law, which they consider to be an antidote against societal vices such as corruption and poverty. Most of them seldom realize the repercussions of such a law for those who are not Muslim, for women, and for Muslims who reject enforcement and political application of a religious law.

Looking at interfaith engagements from the lens of law and tradition furthermore exposes the challenges we meet when discussing the role of women. When Christians and Muslims try to find common language concerning this issue, it is often overlooked that we lack joint articulations about the rules of Islamic tradition, law, and jurisprudence which are based on the teachings of the Qur'an. Although many attitudes, expectations, and perceptions within the respective religions can be traced back to common sources such as the Old Testament, nowadays few Christians refer to biblical scriptures directly, for example, as a source for personal status law.[20] When more fundamentalist-oriented or literalist Christians and Muslims meet in the interfaith discussion similar problems arise. By taking their respective holy texts as literal injunctions, both groups engage in boundary setting, compete for influence and power, and actively proselytize to convince others of their spiritual impurity and deviation from right faith. Both aspire to build God's kingdom on earth. For Muslim radicals this is associated with the application of Shari'ah, under which non-Muslims would belong to a restricted community and be excluded from government positions and participation in politics.[21] Naturally, this point cannot be ignored during interfaith meetings.

Initiatives

For the simple reason that Muslims derive guidance concerning worship and law from these legal rules, these discussions need to be included in interfaith engagements. Currently, both sides are missing this point in spite of numerous interfaith Muslim initiatives. Even the leaders of Saudi Arabia, infamous for thier religious intolerance, have entered the interfaith world. Incurring the wrath of al-Qaeda, Saudi King Abdullah met with Pope Benedict XVI on November 6th, 2007, at the Vatican; the goal of his visit was "to promote common religious and moral values in the world."[22] In July 2008 the kingdom held an international interfaith conference in Madrid "to focus on common human values." The meeting—to which Muslim, Christian, Jewish, Hindu, and Buddhist leaders were invited—could not have been held in the kingdom.[23]

The most hailed initiative, a document titled "A Common Word between Us and You," was launched in the fall of 2007 by a group of 138 Muslim leaders. The document urges both Christians and Muslims to honor the core principles of their sacred texts. The unity of God, the necessity of love for God, and the necessity of love of the neighbor are the common ground between Islam and Christianity.[24] Since it appeared, the document has received numerous reactions from Christian and Jewish groups and institutions, while the number of Muslim signatories has risen to 301.

"A Common Word" is based on readings from the Qur'an and the Bible and does not refer to teachings from the law. An alternative project called "Toward a Muslim Theology of World Religions" brings together a group of about twenty Muslim scholars and leaders from all over the world to attempt to construct contemporary Muslim perspectives on the relation with other religions. The underlying philosophy of the project is that in spite of fundamental theological differences between religions, Muslims must recognize "that theologically the existence of a variety of religious worldviews is part of God's plan."[25] During their first meeting in May 2007 at Al Akhawayn University in Ifrane, Morocco, the participants defined nine areas of exploration starting with the area of law and rights. This choice was based on "the contradictions between the doctrinal ideals and practical realities of Islam . . . as applied in Islamic jurisprudence." Christian theologians ignore these considerations but recognize the language and approach of Common Ground, thus perpetuating formats familiar to them. Let us now turn to the Bridge Building project, which aimed at bringing together those who normally do not interact for the purpose of discussing topics that are conventionally overlooked.

The Bridge Building Project

The Bridge Building project brought out several differences between the intra-religious debates within Islam and Christianity. Concurrently it underscored the reality that within communities there are members with open and inclusive attitudes who struggle to find methods and approaches that produce results that are translatable to the daily life of their community. It took place between March 2008 and June 2010. Since its objective was to involve those who are usually excluded from or not interested in interfaith meetings (identified as conservative, fundamentalist, or radical), one of the expected results was that representatives of those groups would be present and would interact. The project evolved over the course of four meetings—three workshops and one international conference. The initiators stressed the importance of choosing issues of common concern that would allow sparring and disagreeing and provide openings into more difficult issues. Thus they chose as a topic the effects of globalization processes on religious developments and worldviews. In order to facilitate the process of discussing these topics from the respective religious points of view, the topic of globalization was broken down into three subtopics that were discussed in separate workshops and featured in the international conference. In each of the workshops thirty-five participants of different backgrounds were invited. Christian and Hindu leaders whose churches and temples had been attacked met for the first time with members of groups whose religious vision allowed for such acts of violence. Among others, the editor of a radical-minded Islamic journal called *Sabili* came face to face with representatives of the groups it regularly targeted, ranging from feminists, to Zionists, to agents of Western supremacy: Christians.

The first workshop, called "Globalization, Media, and Youth Education," allowed participants to get to know each other and find common ground in discussing the negative and positive aspects of globalizing trends. The second one focused on poverty and environmental issues, encouraging exploration of modes of cooperation. The theme of the third workshop—religious symbols and identity—provided room for critical reflection on the conflicts and the ideological chasms that the use and interpretation of religious symbols can create within and among religious communities.

Throughout the project the word *dialogue* was avoided: many of the evangelical Christians attending did not believe in the concept of interfaith dialogue, while representatives from Islamic groups such as the Hizb ut-Tahrir movement considered it to be a dangerous concept imported from the West.[26] Papers read by individuals representing certain religious worldviews were the starting point for plenary discussions that were continued in breakout groups. The organizers scheduled ample time for meals to allow participants to get to know each other better and have further discussions. Over a period of six months, those involved not only started to create new networks, but also developed a growing enthusiasm about the project and requested that the group continue to discuss topics that concerned participants across the board.

The Project in Religiopolitical Context

As I mentioned earlier, the desire to organize the project arose from a concern over the increasing trends of religious violence and polarization within Indonesian society. After the fall of the repressive Suharto regime in 1998, Indonesians rallied together under a desire for more open democracy and less corruption and cronyism. The regime had clung to power but a collapse of the economy forced Suharto out. In a time of social and financial insecurity, many found consolation in their religious life. In the wake of a national search for meaning, Arab-inspired radical Islamic groups arose at the same time that Christian missionaries were increasingly preaching exclusive messages in mainstream and non-mainstream churches. It was in this atmosphere that hope and anxiety became intertwined and a variety of radical, exclusive groups burst to the surface. Awaiting the fall of the regime had provided a superficial sense of religious harmony and tolerance, even though several Islamic groups had been preparing for this day in exile or in secret.

Using the political vacuum and economic chaos, Islamic extremist groups lobbied for the national application of the Islamic law, while others aimed at disrupting intercommunal relations by provoking strife and violence. A lethal cocktail of political and religious lobbying led to high-profile cases of violence—for example, in the Moluccans (2000), central Sulawesi (especially between 1998 and 2001), and the famous disco bombings in Bali (2002). Non-Islamic houses of worship, shrines, and schools became and continue to be regular targets. This reality forced the National Council of Churches (PGI) in Jakarta to open a division that monitors incidences of violence. Between 2004 and 2007 it counted 108 cases of churches that were destroyed, forced to close, or had experienced interruptions or hindrances in conducting worship ceremonies.[27] They also have kept track of harassment cases resulting from enforcement of local Shari'ah rules.

Several of these incidents were provoked by the actions of Christian or Islamic radical groups. Evangelical missionaries from the West and from countries such as Korea built churches without the required permits and disregarded local demographics, culture, and circumstances. Their actions affected the situation of the mainstream indigenous churches whose houses of worship and schools were attacked by radical Islamic groups that couldn't distinguish between denominations. Violence not only occurs toward those of other faiths, but is also prevalent in the conflicts with groups that are considered to be outside of the Islamic mainstream. A prime example of this mechanism is the treatment of the Islamic sect of Ahmadiyah. The persistent violent attacks on its mosques, houses, and followers increased to over one hundred when the Indonesian government quasi-banned it in June 2008 due to pressure from extremist Muslim groups.

One of the problems facing Indonesia is that the state does not protect those under attack but rather endorses the violence "by commission and omission," according to the head of the think tank Setara, which promotes freedom of religion.[28] In the final analysis, the public and political realms have become platforms where religious actors vie for power, which has resulted in inter- and intra-religious competition and an escalation of violent incidents during the year 2008.[29]

Discussions

With these communal challenges at the forefront of everyone's mind, the organizers of the Bridge Building project chose the general topic of globalization in an attempt to expose underlying motives and patterns of thinking. While participants mostly agreed about general human conditions, some issues revealed persistent fissures in mindsets and worldviews. These divisions, for example, concerned the influence and nature of globalization and were surprisingly more pronounced within the respective religions than across religions.

Difference especially came to the fore in an international conference to which outside speakers were invited. A controversial issue was the nature of globalization itself: some considered it to be an invasive monolithic system born in the West that had to be resisted by a counter-system, whereas others viewed it as consisting of different and disparate movements and influences that are produced not only by Western countries but also other parts of the world. An example of the latter would be the outward spread of Wahhabi Islam from Saudi Arabia. During the workshop, participants agreed that the main challenges caused by globalization were the media and education, which shape the moral religious views of youth. They also concluded that religion "in popular media may invite criticism, but it may also be seen as a strategy to utilize globalization to spread religious messages."[30] Groups such as Hizb ut-Tahrir, in fact, thrive on the tools of globalization that allow them to maintain Web sites and to spread a unified message globally. The most prevalent concern of more fundamentalist minds—especially Muslim and Christian—was globalization's influence on morality. For example, Ismail Yusanto, spokesperson of Hizb ut-Tahrir Indonesia, argued that globalization was a new form of Western imperialism that subjected countries to neoliberalism and unbridled capitalism. According to him, globalization knows no morality, and promotes abortion, homosexuality, and lesbianism.[31]

While fundamentalist-minded Christians could agree with Hizb ut-Tahrir's views, the ones most concerned about this definition and point of view were Muslims who defined themselves as moderate. For example, in her response to Ismail Yusanto's presentation, Lily Munir Zakiyah, an activist for women's rights, fiercely objected to this assessment. She pointed out that Mr. Yusanto presented globalization as if it robbed individuals of their agency and ability to choose. As an example she mentioned the Internet, whereby "movies and pornography can be accessed and so can the Qur'an and the hadiths."[32]

Apart from destroying moral values, in Mr. Yusanto's view, globalization introduces a system that seeks to destroy Islam with its ideals of democracy, pluralism, human rights, and the free market economy. He and like-minded individuals saw as the only antidote to this possible destruction the application of a new system in which a caliph enforces the Shari'ah and adopts an Islamic economic system. While non-Muslim participants questioned what their status should be in the caliphate, Mrs. Munir Zakiyah voiced the opinion of many Muslims when she objected to this alternative Islamic system. While accepting the Shari'ah as a holy law, she asked if the goal was to apply the Shari'ah as a political weapon or as a divine law that "includes norms and values of justice, equality, freedom, humanity, etc." Women activists consider the Shari'ah a weapon in political competitions that threaten women's rights and co-opt women's bodies as the highly visible symbols upon which the Shari'ah is enforced. They do not reject the Shari'ah, which they consider to represent divine guidance, but believe in a law that is not static and is compatible with basic human rights.

This essay conveys only a fraction of the four meetings but illustrates the diversity of opinions among those present. Discussing the role of Shari'ah and jurisprudence belongs to the core of Islamic theology, while non-Muslims see Islamic law as a fearful instrument. The difference in mindset is about how to approach the forces of globalization: through a comprehensive counter-system or via disparate individual actions that create new openings for interfaith engagements. After the second workshop that dealt with the influence of globalization in terms of poverty and the environment, the participants concluded that in order to combat the negative effects of globalization, religious communities should be encouraged to create alternatives by searching for new forms and methods. This exercise of searching together would involve inter- and intra-religious engagements and include theological and non-theological reflections.

Not shying away from controversial and difficult topics helped create new spaces for participants to investigate alternative approaches. Asking honest questions about the other's beliefs and convictions and deliberating the religious and social consequences of the application of certain ideologies not only creates awareness about the other's position but also creates a new level of attention and respect that leads to the formation of alternative networks. Since several of the participants were religious and communal leaders, seeds for future peacemaking were planted. Addressing the repressive aspects for non-Muslims living under nationally enforced Islamic law also opens up venues to discuss the basic rights these groups should enjoy.

Women's Activism

Women's Concerns

A challenge for the project's organizers was to find a gender balance. Several of the more fundamentalist groups failed to send female representatives. Indonesian Muslim women, however, are deeply engaged in a form of dialogue that considers the reinterpretation of Islamic law and jurisprudence as vital for the protection of women's rights. In their view, discussions of rights should be translated into national laws that allow women to seek justice via the court system. This form of advocacy has a long tradition that I have described elsewhere and that has gained in importance with the onset of pro-Shari'ah groups.[33] Although enforcing Shari'ah on a national level has failed, local districts have the freedom to introduce limited Shari'ah rules. The majority of these rules affect women's freedom to move by enforcing curfews imposed on them, and the question of requiring veiling. In certain areas these rules are applied to non-Muslim women as well. Christian students in state schools in Padang, in a district in North Sumatra where Shari'ah was introduced, were forced to wear the Islamic veil to class.[34]

The activities of women resisting religious rules considered to be arbitrary, restrictive, and harmful to women can become a test case for the protection of several rights—those of Muslim and non-Muslim women, and those of freedom of religion. In this context I will illustrate my point with two short examples: one of human trafficking and one of domestic violence.[35] On the surface these projects seem outside the purview of interfaith activities, but actually they show how intra-religious debates can in fact strengthen the fight against these activities.

Human Trafficking

Human trafficking is a modern-day form of slavery. Its root causes are poverty, and, especially after the economic crisis that hit Asia in 1998, stories of maltreatment, exploitation, rape, and virtual imprisonment of migrant workers in Arab Gulf countries and Malaysia started to flood Indonesia. Eighty percent of the victims are women between the ages of thirteen and seventeen.[36] In 2000, the government signed the international protocol to prevent transnational human trafficking but neither undertook official action to stop it nor passed official laws penalizing it.

In 2001, the issue came to the attention of a Muslim women's group called the Fatayat NU. They belong to the organization for unmarried women affiliated with Indonesia's largest Islamic organization, the Nahdlatul Ulama. The Fatayat NU learned that ruthless middlemen recruited young teenage girls from small villages.[37] Some of these girls were given false identity papers and had as their only original source of identification a Fatayat membership card.[38] Traffickers often used corrupt village heads and gullible Muslim leaders to act as intermediates.[39] By 2002, the Fatayat launched an anti-trafficking campaign that in August 2006 culminated in the official request of a fatwa from their parent organization, the Nahdlatul

Ulama. Cooperating with several other organizations such as the interreligious Indonesian Women's Coalition for Justice and Democracy (KPI) and the International Organization for Migration (IOM), the Fatayat organized public discussions and workshops to raise awareness of the issue among religious and community leaders.[40]

The Nahdlatul Ulama granted the requested fatwa that condemned all types of exploitation of women, required officials (police and religious leaders) to prevent it, forbade all types of illegal marriage (temporary or secret), and warned religious leaders that without realizing it they could be facilitating the practice. This fatwa makes clear that the prevention of trafficking is not only a civic duty but also a religious one. An Islamic think tank called the Fahmina Institute followed up with an in-depth study on the anti-trafficking *fiqh*, positioning it within the debates for human and women's rights, with Qur'an 4:58 and 16:90 as a basis.[41]

Muslim and non-Muslim women alike have become victims of human trafficking. Raising awareness about their plight and lobbying for the introduction of laws that make it punishable started as an intra-Islamic movement but was adopted by organizations of non-Muslim women. Within the Indonesian context, women had to use religious arguments in order for the problem to be taken seriously. Thus a basic human rights concern had to be framed in religious terms, especially with reference to the Qur'an and law, in order to be reinterpreted in human rights language. As Indonesia is a country where Muslims are the vast majority, it had to be Muslims who took up and developed this cause. If non-Muslim groups had tried to advance it, they likely would have been ignored or accused of supporting an issue that was "Western" and "un-Islamic."

Domestic Violence

Elsewhere I have discussed similar projects that at first glance seem fully Islamic but actually turn out to be open venues for interreligious activities and advocacy for women's rights and protection.[42] Although Muslim women seem to be the prime targets of radical Muslim efforts to change the public mindset concerning the role and position of women, in the long run such a change in public opinion affects all women, regardless of religious status. Attitudes concerning women's capacities and agency find common denominators in local and national cultures. Although resting on different religious sources, the Indonesian male church leaders' essentialist views of women's inferiority dovetail those of male Muslim leaders. In reality, Indonesian society is undergoing several changes that develop in parallel and overlapping patterns. Traditional gender ideologies exist alongside new ones. Women's access to higher education, modern technologies, global communications, and health care has advanced their positions in society. At the same time, Islamist propaganda still urges women to return to traditional housebound duties of mother and housewife.

The subject of domestic violence illustrates the overlap of local and religious cultures, while also showing how radical Islamist ideas can influence public opinion. Domestic violence is widespread in Indonesia; surveys show that within families 23.3 percent of women and girls are physically abused, and 48 percent suffer from emotional abuse.[43] It was not until 2004 that a national law was passed allowing victims of domestic violence to bring their case to court.[44] Yet the issue of domestic violence remains a heavy taboo. Double sexual standards and ambiguous gender expectations remain the norm in Indonesia, and only 10 percent of abused women actually find the courage to accuse their husbands formally.[45]

Based on Qur'an 4:34, "As to those women on whose part ye fear disloyalty and ill-conduct, admonish them (first), (next), refuse to share their beds, (and last) beat them (lightly)," many Muslim men believe it to be a God-given right to beat their wives, thus prompting women to frequently accept abuse in honor of his religious right to punish her. When spousal abuse is accepted by part of society, the cultural norm will override teachings from other religions. Again with the Muslim majority in mind, it had to be Muslims opening up this discussion. A widespread concern about the plight of victims of domestic abuse led in 1993 to the opening of Rifka Annisa, a center for battered women. The center was founded by a group of women activists representing several Muslim organizations.

They opened up discussions about various forms of physical, emotional, and psychological spousal abuse, including profoundly taboo topics such as marital rape. According to the legal Islamic interpretations of a wife's duties, marital rape is an impossible category since it is her duty to satisfy the husband's sexual needs. The reaction of the current female Minister for Women's Empowerment, who expressed that raising such issues was against "Indonesian culture," showed how unmentionable these topics were.[46]

While analyzing and decoding the Islamic injunctions that had influenced the attitudes concerning domestic violence, the activists opened up discussions about the many ambiguous gender expectations in Indonesian society. These intra-Islamic debates have become venues for interreligious activities since Indonesian Christian, Hindu, and Buddhist women face the same expectations. For example, in her monograph about Christian women in Indonesia, Frances Adeney describes similar mechanisms of double burdens and ambivalent attitudes and expectations toward women in the church. The quote by a woman pastor who wonders if "Christian influence actually harmed women" underscores the complex interaction between religion and culture.[47] Women of all faiths meet in platforms such as the Indonesian Women's Coalition for Justice and Democracy where they advocate for women's rights. Although not given the label of "interfaith or interreligious," these joint activities create solid networks between individuals and groups that help prevent the future breakdown of communal relations.

Conclusion

The three Indonesian projects I describe in this essay might seem far removed from our reality in the West, as they were launched in a country where 87 percent of the population is Muslim and occurred as a reaction to external circumstances at a time when the social, political, and economic circumstances were in constant flux. I chose them not only to illustrate the importance of broadening the interfaith dialogue beyond theological exchanges, but also to show how, in relation to Islam, their theological content differs from that in Christian discourses.

The architects of the projects described were building on a long tradition of interfaith engagement and advocacy for human rights and women's rights. Some of the interfaith discussions had equally started as theological exercises, for example, by comparing injunctions from the Bible and the Qur'an, and discussing the Trinity. In finding different approaches in response to new social and political realities, they built on their extensive experience in these engagements.

The Bridge Building project set out to involve new actors in the interfaith discussions, which would automatically lead to the opening of new areas of discussion. Although many used the familiar format of presenting papers, fierce debates could take place about the impact of the ideas presented. Two very different mindsets met: those whose ideologies implied restrictions of religious freedom, and those whose freedom would be taken away if those ideologies were to be enforced. As the different groups talked about what insulted their sensibilities and how they imagined a future together, these meetings moved from the level of polite encounters to wake-up calls for all involved. The hope is that within their respective movements and organizations those present will move from interreligious discussions to intra-religious ones and serve as counter-voices to discourses that are often formed in isolation without any thought about potential harm or repercussions for other groups.

As this example shows, in certain localities, interfaith exchanges can serve as foundations for future regulations that help protect women. In order to protect the position and rights of women, regardless of their religion, the women went through a reverse process: from intra- to interreligious debates and advocacy. Part of the discussion had to be a close reading of the Islamic law and jurisprudential tradition, which reflected the prevalent ideas of local culture and thus influenced the lives of Muslim and non-Muslim women. By working together on the issues of human trafficking and domestic abuse, women created strong interorganizational and interpersonal networks that will serve as foundations for other future interreligious activities. At the same time, they developed new interpretations of Islam—a new kind of Islam—that prepares them for living in a globalized world where peoples of different faiths are more interconnected than ever before.

Notes

1. Diana L. Eck, *A New Religious America: How a "Christian Country" Has Become the World's Most Religiously Diverse Nation* (San Francisco: HarperOne, 2002).

2. Robert Louis Wilken, "Christianity Face to Face with Islam," *First Things*, January 2009.

3. Tore Lindholm, "Philosophical and Religious Justifications of Freedom of Religion or Belief." In *Facilitating Freedom of Religion or Belief: A Deskbook*, ed. Tore Lindholm, W. Cole Durham Jr., and Bahia G. Tahzib-Lie, 19–61, citation at 31 (Leiden: Nijhoff, 2004).

4. Ibid., 27.

5. Christoffer H. Grundmann describes the ideal situation by probing the term "convivencia," living togetherness, thus: "It is a critically qualified, anti-hierarchical concept which renounces any form of superiority." "Living with Religious Plurality: Theological Reflections on the Interreligious Dialogue." Paper presented at the pre-AAR Conference on Interreligious Dialogue, Lutheran Theological Seminary at Chicago (LTSC), October 31, 2008.

6. William Dyrness, "Islamic, Buddhist and Christian Imaginaries: 'Now I See What You Mean.'" Paper presented at the International Conference on Globalization:

Challenges and Opportunities for Religions, CRCS & ICRS, June 30–July 3, 2008, Yogyakarta, Indonesia. Dyrness builds on the work by Roberto Goizueta, *Caminemos con Jesús: Toward a Hispanic/Latino Theology of Accompaniment* (Maryknoll, NY: Orbis, 1995).

7. For more information about this initiative, see: Narrative Report "Globalization: Challenges and Opportunity for Religion." Three Progressive Workshops and an International Conference. March–July 2008, Yogyakarta, Indonesia. Organized by Center for Religious and Cross-cultural Studies (CRCS), Graduate School, Gadjah Mada University, and Indonesian Consortium for Religious Studies (ICRS), Gadjah Mada University, State Islamic University Sunan Kalijaga, and Christian University Duta Wacana, Sponsored by the Oslo Coalition and Hivos. (Unpublished Report, November 2008), the website of the Oslo Coalition: http://www.oslocoalition.org/indonesia_bbd_conference.php.

8. There are multiple works and thinkers all over the Muslim world trying to rethink Islamic law and teachings in the contemporary world. In the United States, among others, Khaled Abou El Fadl's writings question the authoritarian voices of literalist Muslims. See, for example, his *Speaking in God's Name: Islamic Law, Authority and Women* (Oxford: Oneworld, 2001). Abou El Fadl is part of a group of Muslims who indentify themselves as progressive and whose initial voices are gathered in *Progressive Muslims: On Justice, Gender and Pluralism*, ed. Omid Safi (Oxford: Oneworld, 2003).

9. October 28, 1965; for the entire document, see the Vatican Web site: http://www.vatican.va/archive/hist_councils/ii_council/documents/.

10. World Council of Churches Office on Interreligious Relations, "Striving Together in Dialogue: A Muslim-Christian Call to Reflection and Action," *Islam and Christian-Muslim Relations* 12.4 (2001) 481–88. Also see the document "Ecumenical Considerations for Dialogue and Relations with People of Other Religions: Taking Stock of 30 Years of Dialogue and Revisiting the 1979 Guidelines." Online: http://www.oikoumene.org/index.php?id=3445.

11. For example, see the overview given by Michael L. Fitzgerald, Pontifical Council for Interreligious Dialogue, "Christian Muslim Dialogue—A Survey of Recent Developments," April 10, 2000. Online: http://sedosmission.org/old/eng/fitzgerald.htm. See also Pim Valkenberg, *Sharing Lights On the Way to God: Muslim-Christian Dialogue and Theology in the Context of Abrahamic Partnership* (Amsterdam: Rodopi, 2006).

12. John Hick, *God and the Universe of Faiths: Essays in the Philosophy of Religion*, 2nd ed. (London: Oneworld, 1993) viii–ix.

13. Paul Knitter, *No Other Name? A Critical Survey of Christian Attitudes toward the World Religions* (Maryknoll, NY: Orbis, 1985); Paul Knitter, *One Earth, Many Religions: Multifaith Dialogue and Global Responsibility.* (Maryknoll, NY: Orbis, 1995).

14. Catherine Cornille, *The Impossibility of Interreligious Dialogue* (New York: Crossroad, 2008.)

15. Ursula King, *The Search for Spirituality: Our Global Quest for a Spiritual Life* (New York: BlueBridge, 2008) 74, 75.

16. Paul Griffiths, "Why We Need Interreligious Polemics," *First Things* 44 (1994) 31–37. Online: http://www.firstthings.com/article.php3?id_article=4467.

17. Hyo-Dong Lee, "Interreligious Dialogue as a Politics of Recognition: A Postcolonial Rereading of Hegel for Interreligious Solidarity," *The Journal of Religion* 85 (2005) 555–81; Anselm K. Min, "Dialectical Pluralism and Solidarity of Others: Towards a New Paradigm," *The Journal of Religion* 65 (1997) 587–604.

18. Fatimah Husein, *Muslim-Christian Relations in the New Order Indonesia: The Exclusivist and Inclusivist Muslims' Perspectives* (Bandung: Mizan, 2005) 29–31.

19. See Maurits Berger's "Public Policy and Islamic Law: The Modern *Dhimmi* in Contemporary Egyptian Family Law," *Islamic Law and Society* 8 (2001) 88–136, for an illustration of the law concerning non-Muslim citizens in Egypt.

20. For excellent illustrations of this point, see, for example, *Eve and Adam: Jewish, Christian, and Muslim Readings on Genesis and Gender*, ed. Kristen E. Kvam, Linda S. Schearing, and Valarie H. Ziegler (Bloomington: Indiana University Press, 1999).

21. See, for example, the discussion on the Muslim Brotherhood in Gehad Auda's "The 'Normalization' of the Islamic Movement in Egypt from the 1970s to the Early 1990s." In *Accounting for Fundamentalisms: The Dynamic Character of Movements*, ed. Martin E. Marty and R. Scott Appleby (Chicago: University of Chicago Press, 1994) 386–89.

22. Georg Evers, "Trends and Developments in Interreligious Dialogue," *Studies in Interreligious Dialogue* 18.2 (2008) 228–42 (here 233).

23. Simon Henderson and Jasmine El-Gamal, "Saudi Arabia: Interfaith Talks Abroad, Intolerance at Home," The Washington Institute, July 15, 2008. Online: http://www.washingtoninstitute.org/templateC05.php?CID=2912.

24. The document's official Web site provides the original texts and signatories, the names of those who signed after it came out, and the many reactions from Christian and Jewish groups and institutions. See http://www.acommonword.com/index.php?lang=en.

25. Vincent J. Cornell, Emory University, Project Director, "Abridged Conceptual Summary Report of Conference at Al Akhawayn University, Irane, Morocco, May 27–30, 2007." Unpublished report. I am grateful to Vincent Cornell for his generously sharing the unpublished report with me.

26. See, for example, the conference contribution by the Hizb ut-Tahrir spokesperson in Indonesia: Muhammad Ismail Yusanto,"Globalization, Poverty, and Roles of Religion: Response of Hizb ut-Tahrir." Unpublished paper read at the international conference "Globalization: Challenges and Opportunities for Religions," Yogyakarta, June 30–July 3, 2008. For information about the Hizb ut-Tahrir, see http://english.hizbuttahrir.org/. For the Web site of its Indonesian branch, see http://hizbut-tahrir.or.id/.

27. "Daftar Gereja/Rumah Ibadah yang ditutup, dirusak dan mengalami kesulitan untuk melakukan Ibadah Periode 2004–2007" (List of churches and house churches that were closed, destroyed, or experienced difficulties in holding worship for the period of 2004–2007).

28. "Religious Intolerance Getting Worse, Says Report," *Jakarta Post*, January 14, 2009. For the Web site of the Setara Institute, see http://www.setara-institute.org/.

29. The reports of the two think tanks for freedom of religion, the Wahid Institute and the Setara Institute, indicate the same trend of increased violence: "Report on Freedom of Religion. Indonesia 2008. Siding and Acting Intolerantly: Intolerance by Society and Restriction by the State in Freedom of Religion/Belief in Indonesia," Setara Institute, Jakarta, January 13, 2009. Online: http://www.setara-institute.org/content/siding-and-acting-intolerantly. And the report of the Wahid Institute: "Laporan Tahunan The WAHID Institute 2008 Pluralisme Beragama/Berkeyakinan di Indonesia" (Annual Report of the Wahid Institute, 2008. Pluralism of Religion and Belief in Indonesia), Jakarta, December 18, 2008. Online: http://www.wahidinstitute.org/Dokumen/Detail/?id=22/hl=id/laporan-tahunan-the-wahid-institute-2008-pluralisme-beragama-berkeyakinan-di-indonesia.

30. See "Narrative Report: Globalization: Challenges and Opportunity for Religions."

31. Muhammad Ismail Yusanto, "Globalization, Poverty, and Roles of Religion."

Paper read at Bridge Building Conference, Yogyakarta, 2008.

32. Lily Zakiyah Munir, "Responses to Presentations of Hizb ut-Tahrir's Mr. Ismail Yusanto and JRK's Sandyawan Sumardi on Globalization, Poverty and Roles of Religion." Paper read during the Bridge Building Conference, Yogyakarta, 2008.

33. Pieternella van Doorn-Harder, *Women Shaping Islam: Reading the Qur'an in Indonesia* (Urbana: University of Illinois Press, 2006.)

34. See, for example, the article by Mathias Hariyadi, "Catholic Students Forced to Wear the Islamic Veil," September 17, 2007. Online: http://www.asianews.it/index.php?l=en&art=10318.

35. Part of this material was published in "Controlling the Body: Muslim Feminists Debating Women's Rights in Indonesia," *Religion Compass* 2.6 (2008) 1021–43.

36. Hartian Silawati, et al., *Nightmare in Border Areas: A Study on Child Trafficking in Indonesia for Labour Exploitation* (Yogyakarta: Rifka Annisa, 2004) 26.

37. Editorial page in *Suara Fatayat,* 1/1.

38. Interview of researcher Maryam Fithriati by Monika Arnez, November 10, 2006. I thank Monika Arnez for sharing this information with me.

39. Nur Rofiah, "NU Menyikapi Trafiking" (NU takes a stance on trafficking), *Suara Fatayat* 1 (2006) 18–22 (here 18).

40. See, for example, the Web site of the Women's Coalition: http://www.humantrafficking.org/organizations/121.

41. Q. 4:58: "Allah doth command you to render back your Trusts to those to whom they are due," and Q. 16:90: "Allah commands justice, the doing of good, and liberality to kith and kin, and He forbids all shameful deeds, and injustice and rebellion: He instructs you, that ye may receive admonition."

42. Pieternella van Doorn-Harder, "Controlling the Body: Muslim Feminists Debating Women's Rights in Indonesia."

43. Mohammad Hakimi, et al. *Silence for the Sake of Harmony: Domestic Violence and Women's Health in Central Java, Indonesia* (Yogyakarta: CHN-RL GMU, 2001) 23, 24.

44. *Tindak Pidana Kekerasan terhadap Perempuan dan Anak* (Criminal acts of violence against women and children), ed. Rifka Annisa (Yogyakarta: Rifka Annisa, 2006) 38. The law follows the CEDAW definitions of domestic violence describing its possible domains as physical, sexual, psychological, political, and economic.

45. Interview with Elli Nurhayati, director of Rifka Annisa, July 24, 2007.

46. Quoted in Susan Blackburn, *Women and the State in Modern Indonesia* (Cambridge: Cambridge University Press, 2004) 203.

47. Frances S. Adeney, *Christian Women in Indonesia: A Narrative Study of Gender and Religion* (Syracuse: Syracuse University Press, 2003) 65.